MEDIA NARRATIVES ON HATE SPEECH IN NIGERIA

MEDIA NARRATIVES ON HATE SPEECH IN NIGERIA

Aondover Eric Msughter

GALDA VERLAG 2023

Bibliografische Information der Deutschen Nationalbibliothek
Die Deutsche Nationalbibliothek verzeichnet diese Publikation in der Deutschen
Nationalbibliografie; detaillierte bibliografische Daten sind im Internet über
https://dnb.de abrufbar.

© 2023 Galda Verlag, Glienicke
Neither this book nor any part may be reproduced or transmitted in any form or
by any means electronic or mechanical, including photocopying, micro-filming,
and recording, or by any information storage or retrieval system, without prior
permission in writing from the publisher. Direct all inquiries to:
Galda Verlag, Franz-Schubert-Str. 61, 16548 Glienicke, Germany

ISBN 978-3-96203-302-6 (Print)
ISBN 978-3-96203-303-3 (E-Book)

DEDICATION

This book is dedicated to communication scholars and professionals in Nigeria and the diaspora.

FOREWORD

Developments in the mediascape, especially with the introduction of social media revealed a widening of the base of those who can participate in the public sphere. It would seem that such free and unfettered expression from diverse voices in society is a positive step, assuring the enrichment of the ideal democratic culture. This view is yet to be ascertained given the unrelenting incidents of hate speech in the Nigerian society. Does the freedom that facilitates wide-based participation in the public sphere, also undermine democratic culture by accommodating hate speech, the fear of which would constitute hindrance to participation in public discussions? How can something so vile arise from conditions which are otherwise so ideal? With its attention to Hate Speech in Nigeria, this book is poised to contribute to the tackling of an-all-important puzzle.

It is important to understand how hate speech is generated, its antecedents and consequences in society. The Nigerian society with its fledgling democratic culture has its peculiar experiences which could be rather confounding. Politics in Nigeria is an intense struggle for political power among politicians and their political groups or parties. More worrisome than partisan rivalries are the ethno-centric, sectional, religious colourations that characterise the struggle for political supremacy. These are clear threats to the continued integrity of a nation as diverse as Nigeria. Worse still is the inter-generational dimension to expressions of hate speech which manifested most recently and defies known cultural restraints. Evidently, the spread of hate speech portends great dangers for democracy.

Hate speech is inimical to political stability, as it is to individuals and groups. At the individual, inter-ethnic and religious communities and other levels, expressions of discrimination and hatred diminish trust, respect, cohesion and democratic values. The complex, diverse and globalised nature of the 21st century society further accentuates the challenge. With the rise of populism globally, the occurrence of hate speech as a global phenomenon is also evident. Toxic messages permeate national boundaries. That being the case, this book about the Nigerian experience should be instructive to readers from other shores. Managing the potentials of the media in their ability to spread hate speech through news reports and other forms deserves scholarly attention.

It can be argued that hate speech is chiselling away at the very bedrock of journalism and media practice. The argument for freedom in the media as an extension of freedom of speech needs to be brought under scrutiny. The author's initiative is thus most commendable and should be encouraged. His call for a socially responsible journalistic practice in the news media as a self-regulatory approach against the spread of hate speech should be supported. For this reason, I wholeheartedly recommend *Media Narratives on Hate Speech in Nigeria* to you. We all have a charge to respond to regardless of our academic station – as university and polytechnic undergraduates, teachers, media professionals, media entrepreneurs, researchers and interested readers.

Aondover has challenged us all to attend to an inescapable problem. Do take up the gauntlet. Enjoy the read, and as you do, give serious thought to the manner in which 21st century mediascape can be sanitised and democratic cultures assured.

Professor Oluyinka Esan
Department of Mass Communication
Caleb University, Lagos, Nigeria

PREFACE

Hate speech is among the most significant communication issues that preoccupy the agenda of relevant governmental agencies and media analysts in contemporary Nigeria. It is an unfortunate phenomenon that manifests in the public sphere, and is fast threatening the fragile democracy which the country is struggling to consolidate. Hate speech has become one of the biggest obstacles to democratic consolidation in Nigeria. The rate at which it is being perpetuated by key actors in the political scene is alarming, and its effects diffuse into the entire political system, making it capable of jeopardizing the struggle to consolidate the fragile democracy in the country. Today, most media houses in the country have condescended so low, and have given into the temptation of carrying messages that contain hate and dangerous speech, against the codes of conduct that guide journalism practice in the country. Sensationalism and the drive to sell media content are among the major reasons that entice media organizations to deviate from prescribed codes, and engage in unethical practices such as dissemination of hate speech.

Within this context, Chapter One examines perspectives on hate speech in Nigerian context. It was established in the Chapter that Nigeria as a country is unique in its nature and composition. Hate speech is on the rise in Nigeria, and finds expressions in two major factors that nurture and sustain its continuous existence, namely politics and ethno-religious conflicts.

Chapter Two interrogates the meaning and dimension of hate speech, determinants of hate speeches, and consequences of hate speech. In this direction, hate speech is any speech that attacks a person or group on the basis of attributes such as gender, ethnic origin, religion, race, disability, or sexual orientation.

Issues regarding press in Nigeria constitute the major argument in Chapter Three. The Chapter submits that the history of the media in Nigeria is linked to the political development of the nation. During the colonial era, the attention and efforts of the country's emerging press were generally focused on how to chase away the colonialists through fast-tracking the process of decolonization.

Chapter Four avers that election in any country of the world is not something that can be handled with levity. It determines how and where the country will head in terms of education, economy, infrastructure to mention but a few as this is the process of electing able and competent leaders to strive the ship of the nation for certain period of time.

Chapter Five establishes that a political campaign is an organized effort which seeks to influence the decision making process within a specific group. In democracy, political campaigns often refer to electoral campaigns, where representatives are chosen or referendums are decided.

Chapter Six examines hate speech and the challenges of nation building. It was established that hate speech is a form of directed speech which rejects the core human rights principles of human dignity and equality and seeks to degrade the standing of individuals and groups in the estimation of society generally.

The manifestation of hate and dangerous speech in Nigeria constitutes the topic of discussion in Chapter Seven. The Chapter asserts that substantial part of the speech are devoted to the historical and current trajectory of Nigeria's development and the challenges; corruption, low literacy rate, infrastructural deficit, citizens' alienation and mistrust for government, poor governance and election fraud are among the issues that fuel hate speech in the country.

Ethical and legal position of hate speech formed a topical issue of discuss in Chapter Eight. There are certain laws in Nigeria that checkmate indiscriminate use of verbal and non-verbal attack on the personality of individuals or group of people.

Chapter Nine articulates that freedom of expression is universally acknowledged as both a fundamental and foundational human right. Freedom of expression is a natural right individuals enjoy, which is enshrined in local legislation and international human rights law.

Chapter Ten is a discussion on the effects of hate speech. In this direction, the effects of political activities in developing countries and particularly Nigeria have shown that hate speech has become more vivid in the successive democratic dispensation than the previous ones thereby keeping the citizens more divided.

In Chapter Eleven, instances and criticism of hate speech in Nigeria was given due consideration. Owing to social diversities, hate and other related speeches tend to vary across time and space and possibly constrain by existential societal realities.

Finally, Chapter Twelve explores theoretical postulation of hate speech and violence in Nigeria. The Chapter interrogates the position of theories to better understand the issue of hate speech. As such, for any suggestions from the reading public for further improvement of the book may kindly be sent to the author. Aondover7@gmail.com or eric.aondover@calebuniversity.edu.ng

ACKNOWLEDGMENTS

Glory and honour to God Almighty for the grace, knowledge, wisdom, understanding, and strength to carry out this task. The author is grateful to the numerous scholars whose works have been cited in this book. It is also my singular honour to sincerely thank Professor Yinka Esan of the Department of Mass Communication, Caleb University, Imota, Lagos, Nigeria, for taking the time to review this book and write the foreword.

CONTENTS

Dedication i
Foreword iii
Preface v
Acknowledgements ix

01 Perspectives on Hate Speech in Nigerian Context 1

02 Meaning and Dimension of Hate Speech 7
       Determinants of Hate Speeches 9
       Consequences of Hate Speeches 10

03 Issues Regarding Press in Nigeria 13

04 Media and Elections in Nigeria 19

05 Political Campaign in Nigeria 23

06 Hate Speech and the Challenges of Nation Building 27

07 Manifestations of Hate and Dangerous Speech in Nigeria 29

08 Ethical and Legal Position of Hate Speech 33

09 Freedom of Speech versus Hate Speech 37

10 The Effects of Hate Speech 43

11 Instances and Criticism of Hate Speech in Nigeria 47

12 Theoretical Postulations of Hate Speech and Violence in Nigeria 51

CHAPTER ONE

PERSPECTIVES ON HATE SPEECH IN NIGERIAN CONTEXT

Universally, the press and politics are generally believed to enjoy a symbiotic relationship. In Nigeria, as well as in modern democratic nations, the press has always functioned as a tool for disseminating information on public affairs, interpreting government policies and programmes, and providing a good platform to engage the citizens for discussion on issues affecting society. The media play a powerful role as intermediaries between political leaders and the public (Suleiman & Owolabi, 2018). Xinkum in Suleiman and Owolabi (2018) observe that the role of the press becomes important, especially in influencing voters' judgments about the candidates and take an informed decision about them. This perhaps explains why media scholars have accepted the economic and political change in society (Oso, 2015).

Up till 1922, the election of public office holders was solely determined by the British Colonialists. However, the Clifford Constitution altered the democratic process in the Nigerian political space as Nigerians were given the opportunity to vote and be voted for in the House of parliament. Realizing the role of the media in the democratic process is why a good number of the pre-independence political parties had a newspaper as an ally, which was considered imperative to the survival of their organisation. Retrospectively, since 1960 when Nigeria gained its independence from the British Colonial ruler till dates various parliamentary, military, and presidential systems of government existed. In a democratic society, elections are mostly the conventional means of electing people into all political offices in the country. Against this background, Oso (2015) observes that the importance attached to the party's newspaper was so enormous that people believe that party organisations were built around the press, rather than around organised members.

In line with Oso's view, the newspaper with its close link to political parties was used to set the political agenda. Newspaper like *Lagos Daily News* (1925) was established by Herbert Macaulay, who formed Nigeria National Democratic Party (NNDP). Nnamdi Azikwe also used the *West African Pilot* (1937) to propagate the evangelism of NCNC in which he was a key stakeholder. Obafemi Awolowo also floated the *Nigeria Tribune*, which had a close link with the Action Group (AG). In the North, the *Northern People's Congress*, in 1949, took over Hausa language newspaper, *Gaskiya Ta fi Kwabo*, and its English language counterpart, *Nigerian Citizen* (later as *New Nigerian*) to advocate, defend and advance its interest. The Federal Government, under the Northern Peoples' Congress (NPC), established the *Morning and Sunday Post*; the Eastern Region (under NCNC) had the *Eastern Outlook*, while the North controlled *Gaskiya* and the *Nigerian Citizen*. Furthermore, Chief Samuel Ladoke Akintola established the *Morning Star* towards the end of his Premiership in the old Western Region.

With the intervention of the military in Nigerian politics on December 31, 1984, the Nigerian mass media witnessed the establishment of magazines, periodicals and soft sells newspapers. These include *The Newswatch, The News, The Tempo*, and *Tell magazines*. Others were indigenous language newspapers like *Alaroye, Gboungboun*, and *Irohin Yoruba*. The magazines in particular concerned themselves with investigative journalism and they also contributed immensely towards constructive criticism and the democratization processes of the ruling military establishment under Babangida, Abacha, and Abdulsalam Abubakar respectively. Ever since, the media have regarded the pursuit of full enthronement and sustenance of democracy and democratic institutions and good governance as its abiding responsibilities.

The Independent National Electoral Commission, (INEC, 2015) report stated that consequent upon the approval of Saturday, March 28, 2015, as the dates for the 2015 president and national assembly elections, the campaign exercise began full-blown. In that regard, 14 political parties and presidential candidates were approved by the Independent National Electoral Commission (INEC) in their news release. The parties included Action Alliance (AA), Allied Congress Party of Nigeria (ACPN), African Democratic Congress (ADC), All Progressive Congress (APC), Kowa Party (KP), The National Conscience Party (NCP), Peoples' Democratic Party (PDP), and Progressive People's Alliance (PPA), among others.

At the peak of the electioneering campaign, the two foremost parties (PDP) and (APC) went berserk by taking enmity to the extreme while maligning and attacking the personalities of each other's presidential aspirants through unbridled use of hate speeches. It became so bad that the entire campaign process was almost turned into a harvest of hatred and incitement of one party against the other instead of selling the individual party manifesto (*The Punch*, June 20, 2017).

Similarly, all over the world, hate speech represents a form of threat to damage the lives of individuals and increase the sense of fear in entire communities (United Nations Committee on the Elimination of Racial Discrimination, 2016). Adibe (2015) states that hate speech is any speech that is used to demean persons based on their identifiers, such as race, gender, sexuality, ethnicity, and predisposing people to acts of violence. He maintains that hate speech employs discriminatory epithets to insult and stigmatize others on the basis of their personal marks of distinction or the kind of groups they belonged to. Kukah (2016) holds a similar view that hate speech is universally used to describe any communication that denigrates people (individuals or groups) based on attributes like their race, ethnicity, gender, disability, sexual orientation, nationality, and religion. Hate speech occurs in various forms ranging from speech, gesture, conduct, writing, or display, which could incite people to violence.

Hate speech is a social problem that if not monitored could lead to far greater consequences including war, public disorder, and disrupt the stability and peaceful coexistence of the nation. In Nigeria today hate speech has become very prominent most especially in the political sphere and it is a strong instrument that can lead to the total disintegration of a nation. Apparently, media practitioners tend to be callous concerning their role as peacemakers; rather they serve as the machinery for promoting disunity, igniting crises, and triggering hatred among members of the society (Alakali, et al., 2017). In general, the description of hate speech tends to be wide, sometimes even extending to embody words that are insulting of those in power or minority groups or demeaning of individuals who are particularly visible in society. At critical times, such as during election campaigns, hate speech may be prone to manipulation; accusations of promoting hate speech may be traded among political opponents or used by those in power to curb dissent and criticism.

This could be the reason why Aondover and Muhammad (2018) establish that the recent trend in journalism malpractice in the country is the dissemination of hate speech and vulgar language. The media fell into the trap of reporting hate speech by quoting directly from interviews, press statements, advertorials, and sometimes from alleged online sources.

Despite the fact that some guiding journalism codes of ethics, such as the Nigerian Media Code of Election Coverage (NMCEC), and even members of the society rejected the use of such messages, hate speech still filled the media landscape. Arguably, hate speeches tend to be more on social media among social media users than conventional media because of the absence of gate-keeping. The prevalence of hate speech in the traditional media is also becoming worrisome in Nigeria. This is because apart from undermining the ethics of the journalism profession, it is contributing to bringing disaffection among tribes, political class, and religion or even among friends in the society. Alakali et al., (2017) observe that the Nigerian public is inundated with negative media usage, such as character assassination and negative political campaigns at the expense of dissemination of issues that help them make informed choices.

The media in Nigeria, as indicated earlier have given coverage to some of these issues that showcase some obvious forms of hate speech. Oriola (2019) maintains that the propagation of political hate speech through news reportage could result in infringement on certain rights of the victims such as the right to be voted for, which determines political attainment. Also, it has the potential to infringe on racial, gender, and religious equality among political actors. Once an individual or group has been portrayed in a manner that promotes discrimination, such a victim may be avoided by members of the public and this could lower the victim's chances of political patronage as in the case of the 2015, 2019, and 2023 general elections in Nigeria.

Popoola (2019) also aligns with the description that it is a globally-endorsed paradigm that the media as an important institution in the democratic process plays a key role during elections. As the Fourth Estate of the Realm, the media provide the platform for narratives and discourses in the service of elections, political negotiations, and other features of the contestations among politicians and other civil organisations involved in election administration. However, problems associated with election reporting and media role in political contestations and machinations, particularly on the African continent, have been a recurrent clog in the wheel of politics in Africa. For instance, in Nigeria, from the 1950s up to the early 1980s, spiraling into the Fourth Republic that started in 1999 and beyond, several election problems that were rooted in perceived mishandling of the electoral process by the media, have occurred in the country. The 1965 parliamentary and 1983 general elections were faced by conflicts with accompanying widespread violence, which resulted in military interventions.

It took nearly two decades for the country to return to the path of democracy after the 1983 crisis. In subsequent elections and the attendant crisis in the country, the media have been identified to have played a somewhat negative role as disseminators and conveyors of reports, images, and analyses about the election activities; while media professionals, reporters on the political beat have also been observed to be unacquainted with certain fundamentals of election reporting. This appears a very crucial issue, given the role that the media are expected to play in fostering democracy (Popoola, 2019). Unfortunately, the seeming unsatisfactory conduct of the media in election reporting is apparent, and somewhat paucity of capacity-building resource materials on election reporting.

This perhaps explains the position of Rasaq et al., (2017) that in Nigeria, particularly, the effects of political activities, which show hate speech have become more vivid in the successive democratic dispensation than the previous years. The deeds of politicians have only amplified the situation negatively and keeping the citizens more divided now than ever signals a great source of anxiety to Nigerians at home and in the diaspora. As noted by Pate and Oso (2017) Nigeria is a multicultural nation of diverse people, multiple identities, and colourful outlooks. It has a population of 215+ Million people, 400+ ethnic groups, two major religions, and dozens of political parties, 36 federating states, and additional complex platforms of diversities. The Nigerian multicultural setting is characterised by diversity, heterogeneity, and pluralism in the cultures, orientations, and attitudes of the people. In other words, it connotes diversity as a fact of life on the grounds of sex, cultural practice, ethnic origin, religious affiliation, ideological stance, political leaning, level of social development, place of habitation, and so on.

Ogbuoshi et al., (2019) maintained that today, the Nigerian polity is so heated from all political divides; there has been a resort to hate speech. There are no arguments as to how politicians have resorted to divisive comments, insinuations, and innuendoes. Not only has this hate speech pitched the North against the South but individual hatred has attained an all-time height in Nigeria. With the uncommon level of hate speech in Nigeria witnessed before, during, and after the 2015, 2019, and 2023 general elections, there is a need for the strengthening of theories and methods in the area, particularly when one views communication (hate speech) as having the capacities and infrastructures of threatening the country's collective existence.

Chapter Summary and Conclusion

Chapter one examine perspectives on hate speech in Nigerian context. It was established in the Chapter that Nigeria as a country is unique in its nature and composition. Hate speech is on the rise in Nigeria, and finds expressions in two major factors that nurture and sustain its continuous existence, namely politics and ethno-religious conflicts. Ethno-religious conflicts have become so pervasive, most of which are politically motivated. The outcome of most of them is wide-scale violence that often results in scores of deaths, destruction of lives and property worth millions of naira, intimidation and displacements of residents, etc. Outbreaks of these conflicts often open the window for dissemination of injurious, hate, dangerous and vituperative speeches that have the capacity of accelerating the conflicts. Hate speech has a damaging effect of souring relationships among the various groups that make up the polity. This becomes more serious a case when such hatred is based on unfounded sentiments and is openly expressed in media.

CHAPTER TWO

MEANING AND DIMENSION OF HATE SPEECH

Over the years, scholars and professionals in the area of journalism, politics, conflict studies and comparative religion have conceptualized hate speech in various ways. The conceptualisation of hate speeches has equally come under different meanings and dimensions. Adibe (2015) defines hate speech as:

> Speech that employs discriminatory epithets to insult and stigmatise others on the basis of their race, ethnicity, gender, sexual orientation, or other forms of group membership. It is any speech, gesture, conduct, writing or display which could incite people to violence or prejudicial action. There are individuals and group in this country who openly relish the freedom of speech to rain insults and abusive words on other by appropriating to themselves the role of ethnic and religious crusaders. The problem is that hate speech is often the gateway to discrimination, harassment and violence as well as a precursor to serious harmful criminal acts. It is doubtful if there will be hate-motivated violent attacks on any group without hate speech and the hatred it purveys (p. 55).

In another terms, Kukah (2016) described hate speech as communication that ridicules a particular person or a group on the basis of race, colour, ethnicity, or other characteristic. It is also a form of speech, gesture or conducts that stimulate incitement, violence or prejudice against an individual or a group. The recommendation of the Committee of Ministers of the Council of Europe issued in 1997 defines hate speech as:

> A group of selected words that shall be understood as covering all forms of expression which spread, incite, promote or

justify racial hatred, xenophobia, anti-Semitism, or other forms of hatred based on intolerance. As a result, it generates stigmas, stereotypes, prejudices and discriminatory practices against those who are constructed as being different (p. 55).

Essentially, hate speeches in the Nigerian context, is a form of speech that:

1. Insults people for their religion;
2. Abuses people for their ethnic or linguistic affiliation;
3. Expresses contempt against people because of their place of origin;
4. Disparages or intimidates women or girls because of their gender;
5. Condones discriminatory assertions against people living with disability;
6. Abuses or desecrates symbols of cultural or religious practices;
7. Denigrates or otherwise ridicules traditional or cultural institutions of other people;
8. Deliberately spread falsehood or rumors that demeans or maligns or otherwise ostracises other people on the basis of religion, ethnicity, gender or place of origin for the accident of one form of disability or the other (Umar, 2015, p. 123).

The United Nations Committee on the Elimination of Racial Discrimination (UNCERD) in Suleiman and Owolabi (2018) note that hate speech includes:

a) All dissemination of ideas based on racial or ethnic superiority or hatred, by whatever means;
b) Incitement to hatred, contempt or discrimination against members of a group on grounds of their race, colour, descent, or national or ethnic origin;
c) Threats or incitement to violence against persons or groups on the grounds in (b) above;
d) Expression of insults, ridicule or slander of persons or groups or justification of hatred, contempt or discrimination on the grounds in (b) above, when it clearly amounts to incitement to hatred or discrimination;
e) Participation in organisations and activities which promote and incite racial discrimination.

According to Neisser in Suleiman and Owolabi (2018), hate speech refers to all forms of communication (whether verbal, written, symbolic) that insult a racial, ethnic and political group, whether by suggesting that they are inferior in some respect or by indicating that they are despised or not welcome for any other reasons. They argued that apart from causing danger of physical assault, hate speech provokes violent reaction.

While contributing to hate speech discourse, Jega in Suleiman and Owolabi (2018) argued that there is strong relationship between campaign of calumny (hate speech) and electoral violence, and, that, as far as history is concerned, elements of these have often characterised electoral campaigns in Nigeria. They painted a graphic picture of this thus:

> Elections in Nigeria have historically been conflict-ridden. The campaigns preceding elections are usually marked by pettiness, intolerance and violence, abduction and in extreme cases, assassinations. Elections and their outcomes typically neither free nor fair and are largely characterised by violations of electoral process (both inadvertently and wilful) by electoral officials (p. 56).

From the above, it is clear that hate speech and electoral violence have strong link, and has been largely responsible for the pre-electoral and even the post electoral controversies and violence in most parts of the world, especially in the third world countries where the hold-on-to-power syndrome is strong or rife.

Determinants of Hate Speeches

According to the Nigeria Civil Society Situation Room (2015), there are elements to be examined before a statement can be considered as a hate speech. They are:

a. *Severity*: hate speech can be identified by the harshness of what is said, the brutality of the harm advocated and the intensity of the communication;

b. *Intent*: another way is to look at the intention of the author of the statement. Was the statement intended to spread racism or intolerant ideas or was it just an attempt to inform the public about an issue of general interest?

c. *Content*: facts contained in the speech including its tone are both important for consideration. Does it require listeners' response with certain actions or inactions? The speakers themselves should be considered, specifically their standing in the context of the audience to whom the speech is directed. The level of their authority or influence over the audience is relevant as this has the potential of conditioning the mind of the audience to take negative action.

d. *Extent*: this refers to the public nature of the speech. For speech to qualify as hate speech, it must have occurred in public. This also means specific audience (general public) or to a number of individuals in a public space.

Consequences of Hate Speeches

By far, the greatest consequence of hate speech is election violence. Fischer in Suleiman and Owolabi (2018) identified different manifestations of election violence and classified them as follows:

i. Pre-election day violence (it occurs during the registration period and can lead to massive disenfranchisement of voters due to psychological fear);

ii. Campaign violence can evolve when major political meetings and rallies are held. This period is the most susceptible to the highest degree of electoral violence;

iii. Election day violence manifest in the forms of burning of election offices and materials including ballot boxes and papers, intimidation of voters, snatching of ballot boxes, rigging and diversion of election materials;

iv. Post-election day violence can also occur hours and days after elections. This can emanate from disputes over election results and the inability of judiciary to handle election dispute fairly. The manner in which election results are announced might also lead to electoral violence.

Chapter Summary and Conclusion

Chapter two interrogates the meaning and dimension of hate speech, determinants of hate speeches, and consequences of hate speech. Hate speech is any speech that attacks a person or group on the basis of attributes such as gender, ethnic origin, religion, race, disability, or sexual orientation. Hate speeches are utterances, typed documents, advertorials, musicals or any form of literature that are used to attack an individual, a group, religious, social, political, business - gender or race. In some countries, hate speech can fall under the law of sedition, incitement to violence, verbal abuse and the likes. Hate speech is any speech, gesture, conduct, writing or display which could incite people to violence or prejudicial action. Essentially, such speeches rob others of their dignity.

The Chapter also articulates that hate speech employs discriminatory epithets to insult and stigmatize others on the basis of their race, ethnicity, gender, sexual orientation or other forms of group membership. It is any speech, gesture, conduct, writing or display which could incite people to violence or prejudicial action. Hate speech is often the gateway to discrimination, harassment and violence as well as a precursor to serious harmful criminal acts. It is doubtful if there will be hate-motivated violent attacks on any group without hate speech and the hatred it purveys.

CHAPTER THREE

ISSUES REGARDING PRESS IN NIGERIA

The history of the early years of the press indicates an absence of ethnic motivations and calculations in the establishment and operations of the Nigerian press. Pate (2015) explains that the early newspapers were mainly published by liberated Africans (Sierra Leoneans and Liberians) who had settled in Lagos and environs. He argues that by the time Nigerians joined the newspaper publishing business at the beginning of the 20th century, there was hardly any ethnic, regional, or other sectional coloration in the philosophy or operation of these newspapers. Thus, the ethnic tendencies commonly found in the content of the press are a latter development that sought to reflect in a relevant manner the various contentions that defined the politics of the nation.

The history of the role of the media in Nigeria is linked to the political development of the nation. During the colonial era, the attention and efforts of the country's emerging press were generally focused on how to chase away the colonialists through fast-tracking the process of decolonization. As noted by Oso (2018) the Nigerian press emerged to challenge, compete with and ultimately displace colonial institutions in the socialisation process. The press acted as a rallying point and a source of inspiration through militant-type reporting that was heavily tilted against the colonial regime.

Most of the newspapers of the period developed into political party organs that championed anti-colonial campaigns and promoted the political relevance and ambition of their leaders. Such militant stance of the press continued after the country's independence in October 1960, with many of the newspapers refocusing their anti-colonially inspired behaviour towards the new national government. As noted by Pate and Jibril (2018) most of them engaged in partisan conflicts and serious bashing of the Balewa led government. In the process, the press got divided along regional lines with individual papers being closely referred to as mouthpieces for particular parties and regions. For instance, the Action Group and the Western Region were associated with the *Daily Express* and the *Nigerian Tribune*; the North and the NPC were linked to the *Gaskiya ta fi Kwabo* and *Nigerian Citizen* (*New Nigerian*), and the *Eastern Region* and the NCNC were associated with the *Pilot* and *The Renaissance*.

Oso (2018) observes that the newspapers were completely immersed in the vortex of partisan politics and were in no position to prepare the people for the challenges of independence. National party newspapers were locked in vicious combat. Perhaps, that was why it was variously argued that the press had played, either by commission or omission, critical facilitative roles in the collapse of the first republic. However, even at that scholars like Pate (2015) and Oso (2018) believe that the media of the time had played some active positive role in sporting the nationalist politicians and political parties to achieve 'respectable progress' in the achievement of independence in 1960; the declaration of Nigeria as a Republic in 1963; the enthronement of democracy as the defining feature of politics and governance in the society as well as the practice of federalism.

According to Pate (2015) with the collapse of the first republic and the subsequent military takeover in 1966 and the intense hostility that followed, some sections of the press rose to the national challenge by assuaging the feelings of the people, particularly in the North and Western regions where they felt hurt by the assassination of political and military leaders from their part of the country. For instance, the *New Nigerian* newspaper, which commenced production a few days before the first coup, wrote in an editorial that it will champion "the vital need for national unity" arguing that "without unity and trust and mutual respect this great country will never find its rightful place." In another editorial during the civil crisis in 1967, the paper submitted that:

> We have got to achieve nationhood in a record time. The British may have created a geographical area called Nigeria but they did not create a nation of Nigerians. Nationhood cannot be achieved in legislative chambers. It must come from the heart of every individual. Every person in the land must play his part. Honesty, hard work, trust, and understanding are all needed (p. 14).

During the civil war, all the newspapers except for those that were in the rebel-controlled Eastern Nigeria supported the war effort. They countered the intense propaganda from the Biafran machinery and forcefully supported the government's handling of the war. For example, the *Daily Times* campaigned continuously during the war period that "Gowon was fighting to keep Nigeria one" (Pate & Jibril, 2018). An editor of the *New Nigerian* during the war period, Mallam Adamu Ciroma recalled that "the years 1966-1970 were the years of political crisis, turbulence, and civil war. Reporters were at the war front before the war began. People were quick to read the writing on the wall. Reporters moved with the troops." Newspapers in the country saw the successful prosecution of the war as the single preoccupation that they had to support for the continued unification of the nation. Even when the war ended, they continued to support the government's cardinal goal of reintegrating the Igbos through its programme of reconstruction, rehabilitation, and reconciliation (Bello, 2015).

After the end of the civil war in 1970, the military continued to rule Nigeria up to 1979 when it handed over to a civilian government that lasted for only four years. During the period, the press had a series of disagreements with the Military government of General Gowon that bordered on issues of accountability and democratization. Eventually, the Gowon regime was overthrown in 1975. He was succeeded by General Murtala Mohammed and later General Olusegun Obasanjo in 1976. Even though the Murtala and Obasanjo regime expressed unhappiness with the conduct of the press in their handling of the Shariah, a debate erupted in the Constituent Assembly and the Constitution Drafting Committee of 1977 and 1978 preparatory to the exit of the military in 1979. The newspapers in the Northern and Southern parts of the country took diametrically and sharply opposing positions that were divisive along religious lines (Bello, 2015).

According to Oso (2018), the debate became acrimonious and threatening to religious peace and national unity that the Head of State had to call for a ceasefire to the raging explosive exchanges in the media. Similarly, another divisive debate on religion was sparked off from 1986 to 1987 during the Political Bureau Report preparation and the circumstances over the membership of the country in the Organisation of Islamic Countries (OIC). Again, the newspapers took dangerously divisive positions with threatening editorials and write-ups, supposedly on behalf of their regions, religions, and sponsors (Batta et al., 2016).

Earlier in December 1983, the Military had, once again, taken over the country. That dispensation lasted up to 1999 when the Military eventually disengaged from the political governance of the nation (Bello, 2015). While the Military generally acknowledged the contributions and even tolerated the excesses of the press towards national unity and integration during the war period, it seemed those in government did not trust the press to be reliable enough to uphold and consolidate national unity and the process of integration thereafter. At several times, the rulers and their agents reminded the media that they are partners in progress that should be guided by the unity and development of the nation. For instance, in 1984, the Information Minister, Group Captain Samson Emeka Omeruah reminded the press that it has "a basic duty to perform in ensuring the peace, unity, progress, and stability of this country. "Our nation is too young to indulge in destructive sensationalism, deliberate mischief and purposeless slants, which only set us back from the path of progress and development" (*New Nigerian*, Aug. p. 8).

President Babangida who ruled for eight years starting from 1985 implored the press to be the "custodians of the good of the society; the barometer of national unity and security; the protector of its moral climate and the defenders of its interest (Pate & Jibril, 2018). However, because of the frustration, anger, desperation, and cynicism that visited the Nigerian middle class during the Babangida period as a consequence of SAP, issues like intellectual dishonesty and ethnic particularism enveloped the nation and called for national disintegration filled the pages of the newspaper. *Tell Magazine*, Jan. 25, in Pate (2015) paints a gloomy picture of the country in 1993 when it wrote that:

> The mood in the nation is now of anomie. A deep malaise pervades the entire land as a function of the crises the nation is facing. The economy is in shambles; the transition programme has yielded a command democracy that holds only the promise of a progressive slight back to our failed past; ethnic and regional antagonism have never been so threatening to condemn us to repeat the bloody aspect of our recent history; various public institutions and social services are on the verge of collapse and the stench of our moral decay is becoming unbearably suffocating. The nation is tottering on a precipice (p. 16).

The return of democracy in 1999 reduced the tension in the land and offered increased platforms for the expression of individual feelings and agitations without necessarily threatening national unity. Accordingly, the attitude of the press also titled more to issues of supporting individuals and communities to make their cases against perceived injustices, marginalization, and resource control, irrespective of the validity of some of them. The press became preoccupied with petty conflicts among the new set of politicians, who in most cases are the sponsors and lords of the papers. In the words of Bello (2015):

> The conduct and performance of the 4th Republic politicians and regimes indicate that they have deviated from the various chequered attempts at democracy, independence, republicanism, federalism, and national unity which characterized the former republics. The 4th Republic politicians do not also seem particularly disposed to the nationalist orientations of the former military regimes towards the promotion of national unity or enhancing the republican status of the country (p. 19).

Specifically, in 2006 and 2007, the attention shifted heavily to fighting the Third Term agenda of President Obasanjo. The fight, though signified the most united voice of the press is fighting a national course, was, however, because many of the sponsors in the press felt cheated by the Third Term attempt. That notwithstanding, it was a resolute voice from a large section of the press in support of a national course with little resort to the usual fault lines. With the Third Term struggle over, the issue of ethno-religious conflicts and the Boko Haram insurgency overwhelmed the country. Again, the media rose to the challenge. The coverage of Boko Haram was massive, initially with some misunderstanding of the complexities of the issues and the attempt to portray the insurgency as an inter-religious war or effort by adherents of one religion to exterminate the others. For some time, one could see evidence of misunderstanding, expression of ignorance, and in many cases resort to the perpetuation of stereotypes in the coverage of Boko Haram terrorism. However, with time, things changed. The press became better equipped in being able to report, analysed, and comment on the subject. Today, the issue of Boko Haram has lessened, and hate speech is dominating in the media.

Chapter Summary and Conclusion

Issues regarding press in Nigeria constitute the major argument in Chapter three. The Chapter remarks that the history of the media in Nigeria is linked to the political development of the nation. During the colonial era, the attention and efforts of the country's emerging press were generally focused on how to chase away the colonialists through fast-tracking the process of decolonization. The Chapter argues that the Nigerian press emerged to challenge, compete with and ultimately displace colonial institutions in the socialisation process. The press acted as a rallying point and a source of inspiration through militant-type reporting that was heavily tilted against the colonial regime.

CHAPTER FOUR
MEDIA AND ELECTIONS IN NIGERIA

Nigeria's electoral history dates back to the colonial period and the media have always featured prominently in the different phases of that history. Reckoning with the fact that elective democracy was introduced in 1919, it suffices to posit that by the time Nigeria held elections in 2023, the country was celebrating many elections (Arogundade, 2019). However, the first 'general election' during the colonial period and in which Nigerians participated was in 1923. In the said election, only four Legislative Seats; three in Lagos and one in Calabar were contested for out of forty-six Council elective seats. This followed the promulgation of the Clifford Constitution (named after Governor Hugh Clifford) in 1922. The four elected were Egerton Shyngle, Eric Moore, and Crispin Adeniyi-Jones of the Nigerian National Democratic Party for Lagos and Kwamina Ata-Amoun, an independent candidate for Calabar (Aondover, 2021).

According to Arogundade (2019), all elections between 1923 and 1959 were under the colonialists, and not until 1964 that the first post-independence elections were held. Subsequent post-independence elections were held in 1979, 1983, 1992, 1993, and between 1999 and now. The 1979 elections marked the transition from the parliamentary system of government to the presidential system. However, Arogundade (2019) notes that given the very huge cost of governance that the current experiment of the presidential system attracts, there have been debates on which system of government is suitable and affordable for the country to run, according to the best global practices.

The long history of elections is also reflected in many constitutions the country has had from the Clifford's in 1922 to the 1979 Constitution, the 1989 Constitution, and the current 1999 Constitution. At the same time, there have also been different Electoral Management Bodies that have superintended over the elections. Among these are the Electoral Commission of Nigeria

(ECN) 1959; Federal Electoral Commission (FEC) 1960-65; Federal Electoral Commission (FEDECO) 1979-83; National Electoral Commission (NEC) 1992; National Electoral Commission of Nigeria (NECON) 1995 and the Independent National Electoral Commission (INEC) 1998 till date.

Arogundade (2019) is of the view that Nigerian elections have often been characterised by violence, notably the western region post-election violence of 1964, code-named Operation *wetie* (soak it with petrol) and similar ones in 1979, 1983, and 1993. That of 1993 followed the annulment of the result of the election held on June 12, which was won by late Moshood Kashimawo Abiola, by the military government of General Ibrahim Babangida. Also, in the 2007 and 2011 elections, there was post-electoral violence in which not less than 800 people were killed in the Northern part of the country (Batta et al., 2016). The elections held in 2015, 2019, and 2023 in the country were equally characterised by the destruction of lives and property as a result of widespread hate speech by the media.

Unfortunately, one of the most worrisome aspects of Nigerian electoral history is that the media in Nigeria have been indicated at various times for contributing to political or electoral tension and cycles of electoral violence in the country. In terms of professional misconduct, the Nigerian media may not have acted differently from the media in other places as this book establishes instances of media misconduct in elections processes. As observed by Arogundade (2019) it is worth underlining that the alleged misconducts occur despite the continual existence of frameworks governing the responsibility of the media in elections and democracy. Media are required to be of good ethical and professional conduct during elections. Among the current statutory frameworks are the Constitution (the overarching statutory framework); the Electoral Act 2010 (as amended) and the Nigeria Broadcasting Code (5th edition). The voluntary and self-regulatory ones include the Code of Ethics of Journalists in Nigeria and the Nigeria Media Code of Election Coverage (revised edition, 2018).

Similarly, political reporting pre-dates Nigeria's independence and is traceable to the pre-independence press, pioneered by the first newspaper in Nigeria, *Iwe Irohin fun awon ara egba ati Yourba* (Newspaper for the Egba and Yoruba People), which made its debut on the 3rd of December, 1859. The media indeed cannot be separated from the political history of Nigeria as some of the Nationalists that fought for independence and some of whom later became political and government leaders were media proprietors and professionals including Herbert Macaulay, founder of *Daily Star*; Nnamdi Azikiwe, founder of *West African Pilot* and Obafemi Awolowo founder of the *Nigerian Tribune*, among others. Thus, Arogundade (2019) remarks that democracy, which is considered the 'best' form of governance, can only thrive with a robust media institution, which, because of its importance, is considered the Fourth Estate of the Realm.

Therefore, Arogundade (2019) maintains that the 1983 elections happened to be the second and the last of the second republic. There was post-election violence in parts of the country following allegations of massive rigging against the then ruling National Party of Nigeria (NPN) by opposition parties, especially the Unity Party of Nigeria (UPN), whose candidate Obafemi Awolowo believed to have been robbed of victory in favour of President Shehu Shagari. The major violence was the then Ondo State where the state media was accused of playing a major role in the targeting of inciting attacks and killing of opposition politicians loyal to the erstwhile Deputy-Governor, Akin Omoboriowo who had decamped to the NPN to challenge the incumbent, Chief Adekunle Ajasin.

As documented in the Resource Manual on Elections and Democratic Accountability Reporting (IPC, 2018) and Nigeria Decides: media, hate broadcast and 2015, 2019, and 2023 elections, the media (especially the state radio and television stations) were used to propagate an atmosphere of fear and hate leading to the violence that marred it and ultimately the demise of the Second Republic. In the reports, at least 70 people were slaughtered in Ondo State during the media-induced electoral violence and Bayo Olupohunda was dismayed that the purveyors of hate campaigns and propaganda in the state media were never investigated and prosecuted for their roles in the violence. The state media in question was the Ondo State Broadcasting Service (OSBC) whose on-air personnel, at the peak of the post-election crisis, abandoned all other forms of programming only to engage in the announcement of the movements of opposition politicians, especially Chief Omoboriowo, often in the Yoruba indigenous language to aid mob attacks on them.

Also, it was in the aftermath of the general elections in 2007 that Mwai Kibaki of the Party of National Unity (PNU) and Ralia Odinga of Orange Democratic Movement (ODM) were the major contenders. Each of them leaned on the respective Kikuyu and Lou ethnic bases. As if the lessons of the Rewandan genocide in 1996 were not learned, the media queued behind either candidate helped to unleash verbal ethnic warfare. Hundred died in the ensuing political violence to the embarrassment of journalists across the world. An international media conference was later held in the country at which the Kenyan journalists admitted to their failings and at which the principles of conflict-sensitive journalism were again espoused. The conference also proclaimed that journalists the world over must understand that their 'tribe' is no other but journalism (Batta et al., 2016).

Chapter Summary and Conclusion

Chapter four submits that election in any country of the world is not something that can be handled with levity. It determines how and where the country will head in terms of education, economy, infrastructure to mention but a few as this is the process of electing able and competent leaders to strive the ship of the nation for certain period of time. It is a vital tool that shapes the fate of any country. Nigeria is a country with different political, religious and ethnic diversities. This is one of the reasons elections in the country are always intense and always generating issues. Many elections have been conducted in the country and they are marred with one negative factor or the other – ranging from election irregularities, violence, hate speeches and the host of others.

In this context, the media recorded numerous hate speeches being sent across them by the enthusiasts of political parties in the country. The Chapter pointed that hate and divisive speeches dominate political rallies as the elections heat up a political space already notorious for its violence. Hate and divisive speeches take on more frightening dimensions online via social media, notably Facebook, Twitter and YouTube by cashing in on the fault-lines: religion and ethnicity. Within this conceptual context, the role of the media in strengthening democratic ethos is fundamental, especially in checkmating the kind of content that can be dish out to the society that can foster development rather than dividing the country.

CHAPTER FIVE

POLITICAL CAMPAIGN IN NIGERIA

Electioneering campaign practices began in the years leading to Nigeria's independence in 1960. However, these campaigns were generally marked by thuggery, ethnic sentiments, and violence among supporters of opposing parties (Omidiora et al., 2019). However, political campaigns became more popular in the country during the third republic as presidential candidates of the Social Democratic Party (SDP) and the Nigerian Republican Convention (NRC) channeled more resources into nationwide political campaigns. By the fourth republic, more creativity, especially through the use of the Internet was introduced into political campaigns, even though electoral campaigns in the fourth republic are still marked by many features of the electoral campaigns of the first republic (e.g. violence and ethnic sentiments). The reasons for this are not implausible; Taiwo in Omidiora et al., (2019) observe that Nigeria, since independence, has been faced with varying levels of socio-political imbalances and crises, all of which contribute to the forms of political discourse that are produced in the polity.

Political campaigns, according to Ukonu (2006), are an organised effort which seeks to influence the decision-making process within a specific group, or environment. This is because it provides that mobilizing force either by an organisation, or individuals with the intent to influence others in order to foster an identified and desire political change. The import of this is that it shows people and particularly, political candidates the ability to sensitise the political community to consider them as potentials and better representatives of the people.

A critical analysis of the above shows that for a political campaign to be able to act effectively as a mobilizing force that will influence the decision of the people, the message contained in the campaign must be intelligible, convincing and attainable. It is in line with this that the author aligns with Suleiman and Owolabi (2018), that:

> … what seems to be very important in any political campaign is the message that is sent to the electorates. A campaign message is an important and potent tool that politicians use to express views and feelings to the public with the intention of reshaping and redirecting the electorates' opinions to align with theirs. The message should be a simple statement that can be repeated severally throughout the campaign period to persuade the target audience or influence voters to act in the candidate's favour. The campaign message ought to contain the salient ingredients that the candidate wishes to share with the voters and these must be repeated often in order to create a lasting impression on the voters. As a matter of fact, good campaigners prefer to keep the message broad to attract the voters. In other words, it calls for appropriate use of language most dignified and intelligible to target audience (p. 54).

In the case of Nigeria, the use of hate speeches in the electioneering has provided a different dimension to the context and background of how elections are conducted in this country.

Literature abounds on the features of political discourse in Nigeria (e.g. Ademilokan 2015; Omidiora et al., 2019, etc) stylistically examines linguistic choices made by one of the earliest politicians in Nigeria, Obafemi Awolowo. The outcome of their studies shows that for rhetorical appeals, metaphors are foregrounded elements in the speeches of the politician.

Similarly, Oladeji in Omidiora et al., (2019) analyses the use of songs in political communication in the Southwestern region of Nigeria. He notes that songs were used to praise political actors and their supporters on the one hand, and, on the other hand, used to express animosity towards opposing political parties or groups. Though he concludes that the use of songs arose because most residents of the region were illiterate, he observes that orality plays a significant communication role in African politics, hence, songs in political discourse may function as necessary alternative modes of communication. Ademilokun (2015) posits that songs in political rally discourse are signifying practices that transcend entertainment to reveal ideological, psychological, and idiosyncratic semiotic implications.

Oha in Omidiora et al., (2019) examines the style of war speeches of General Gowon and Colonel Ojukwu during the Nigerian Civil War and concludes that language is a powerfully persuasive and motivating tool in politics. Adegoju (2015) observes that the June 12 Nigerian elections further indicates that person deixis is a discursive strategy appropriated in the conflicting rhetoric of political figures to control or shape the cognition and actions of their audiences.

Omidiora et al., (2019) maintain that political actors may attempt to re-orient the cognitions of their audience through specific discursive choices. In an analysis of President Jonathan's declaration of his candidacy for his party's presidential primaries, they identify positive-face and negative-face rhetorical strategies which the candidate employed to present himself as a metaphor of change in the Nigeria polity.

Ademilokun (2015) however, sheds light on the problem of political language and truth values. He notes that political advertisements package and market the politician's political image and this may include deftly structured deception and even the use of abusive language, as there seem to be no ethical bounds like these adverts. Ademilokun (2015) likewise observes that politicians make conscious linguistic choices such as code-switching and code-mixing, allusion, and propagandist language during political campaigns to identify with the audience and gain their support. The author concludes that language is central to the presentation of a candidate and his or her manifesto to the public. Hence, discourse remains an effective platform for political expression.

All of these authors examined political discourse in Nigeria from varying linguistic perspectives. This book, however, re-emphasises the place of hate speech in the discourse of political campaigns, asserting that politicians normally used hate speech during political campaigns, which plays significant role in the electioneering process of the Nigerian polity.

Chapter Summary and Conclusion

This Chapter established that a political campaign is an organized effort which seeks to influence the decision making process within a specific group. In democracy, political campaigns often refer to electoral campaigns, where representatives are chosen or referendums are decided. In modern politics, the most high profile political campaigns are focused on candidates for head of state or head of government, often a President or Prime Minister. Political campaigns are as old as civilization. As people became civilized, there was need to have a system that will run the affairs of the different societies we have in the word. Thus, political campaigns become necessities. It is a conscious effort of someone or individuals who seek the support of people or a group of people in order to win an elected post. In politics, campaigns through the media have become an essential tool used amongst candidates contesting for various positions to get the electorates to vote for them. When it is time for election and political campaign in any country, the atmosphere is always very intense. The political sector of the country will witness a heavy shake up and many activities and issues will come to the fore. A political campaign is step in the electoral process of any country and it ushers in the real voting process. The campaign usually determines how the real election will look like.

CHAPTER SIX

HATE SPEECH AND THE CHALLENGES OF NATION BUILDING

Scholars like Ogbuoshi et al., (2019) observe that hate speech is so pervasive in Nigeria that many citizens are susceptible to it. The opposite is that people who usually complain of being insulted by other ethnic groups often use even more hateful words in describing such groups. Thus, they remark that the widening of the social distance among the different ethnicities make up the country and an exacerbation of the crisis in the country's nation-building. Several observations could be made about the interplay between ethnicity, hate speech and the crisis in the country's nation-building project (Aondover, 2022). One, hate speech employs discriminatory epithets to insult and stigmatize others based on their race, ethnicity, gender, sexual orientation or other forms of group membership. This could be the reason why Ogbuoshi, et al., (2019) maintain that it is any speech, gesture, conduct, writing or display which could incite people to violence or prejudicial action.

Adibe (2018) and Oguoshi et al., (2019) articulate that there are individuals and groups in Nigeria who openly relish the freedom to rain insults and profile others by appropriating to themselves the role of ethnic and religious champions. The implication is that hate speech is often the way to discrimination, harassment and violence as well as a precursor to serious harmful criminal acts. This perhaps explains the reason why Adibe (2018) aligns with the description that it is doubtful if there will be hate-motivated violent attacks on any group without hate speech and the hatred it purveys. Secondary, there is nothing wrong in the people celebrating pride in their ethnic and cultural identities as it is not always a manifestation of ethnicity when someone proclaims, "I am a proud *Hausa, Igbo* or *Yoruba*".

Therefore, most ethnic groups across the world feel that their way of life, food, dress, habits, beliefs, values and so forth are superior to those of other groups. There is nothing wrong with this. The boundary between this love for one's ethnic identity (ethnocentrism) and ethnicity (which is conflictual) could however be thin. As noted by Adibe (2018) when people's love for ethnic identify results in seeing other groups as competitors or the reasons why others are not getting what people believe they deserve to get, then there is often recourse to hate speech to vent others frustrations on the out-group. At a point, the love for one's ethnic identify has become conflictual in form and thus; crossed the boundary to ethnicity.

It is important to underline that although ethnicity is rooted in the struggle for the scare societal values political positions, jobs, contracts, scholarship, etc by the various ethnic factions of the Nigeria elite, it has over time acquired an objective character such that it now exist independent of the original causative factors. Similarly, there are group of 'ethnic watcher' whose only vocation appears to be working the arithmetic of which ethnic group gets what, when and how in the proverbial sharing of the 'national cake' (Nwokoro, 2019). As such, the process of nation-building requires conscious efforts from all and sundry, irrespective of political, social or ethnic affinity.

Chapter Summary and Conclusion

This Chapter examines hate speech and the challenges of nation building. It was established that hate speech is a form of directed speech which rejects the core human rights principles of human dignity and equality and seeks to degrade the standing of individuals and groups in the estimation of society generally. All forms of expression which spread, incite, promote, or justify racial hatred, xenophobia, anti-Semitism or other forms of hatred based on intolerance, including intolerance expressed by aggressive nationalism and ethnocentrism, discrimination, and hostility towards minorities, migrants, and people of immigrant origin can be calculated as hate speech. Thus, hate speech constitute a challenge to nation building as such speeches undermine the collective effort and peaceful co-existence of people that can facilitate developmental initiatives.

CHAPTER SEVEN

MANIFESTATIONS OF HATE AND DANGEROUS SPEECH IN NIGERIA

Hate speech and dangerous speeches are often made along some key divides in Nigeria. They include religion, ethnicity, regionalism, political affiliation, among others. Politicians have often deployed religion to either mobilize support for or oppose certain candidates. In the process, their use of language has incited followers to commit violence against others. The charge of apostasy declared against ordinary people, who often were not Muslims, for example has resulted in the killing of many people by mob action (Fatonji et al., 2020).

Political parties are historically organised largely around ethno-cultural associations, which transform into parties. From the pre-independence period, politicians have deployed ethnicity to protect their "home" constituencies even as they try to win other constituencies. More so, discourse within the country tends to polarise the citizens along regional and ethnic lines. The three major ethnic groups of Hausa, Igbo and Yoruba tend to dominate other ethnic groups, though there is a general perception, particularly in the South and Middle-belt of Hausa-Fulani hegemony. That had different ethnic groups, which often leads to separatist agitation, violent militancy and the campaign for resource control and restructuring or true federalism.

There have also been several communal-ethno-religious conflicts in several parts of the country, of which the farmer-herdsmen conflict is the most current and persistent. These conflicts were not originally triggered by hate speech but hate speech has since become the keg with which the fuels for these recurrent conflicts are being ignited. Elsewhere in the country, hate speech has often featured in mobilization by youth in several communal conflicts such as the Ummuleri/Aguleri, Ife/Madakeke, etc. Also, Nigeria's 30 month civil war did not only lead to loss of lives and property, it also left bitter memories that remain a key reference point for hate speech in the country (Fatonji et al., 2020).

Therefore, hate speeches are made to incite the public order or cause disharmony between the government and its various constituents, usually with potentials of violence and published or broadcast in the mass media. However, the term remains widely contested. According to UNESCO (2015), multilateral treaties such as the International Covenant on Civil and Political Rights (ICCPR) have sought to clarify the concept. Yet, "hate speech continues largely to be used in everyday discourse as a generic term, mixing concrete threats to individuals' and groups' security with cases in which people may be simply venting their anger against authority" (UNESCO, 2015, p. 7).

Hate speech is universally used to describe any communication that denigrates a particular person or a group on the basis of race, color, ethnicity, gender, disability, sexual orientation, nationality, religion, or other characteristics. It can be in the form of speech, gesture, conduct, writing, or display. The link between a rise in hate speech and violence is therefore easy to make. Incidentally, the mass media have been found to be the highest purveyor of hate messages (Fatonji et al., 2020). This portends a challenge to the Nigerian democratic process and the desire for a hitch-free election and avoidance of post-election violence.

Jibrin et al., (2017) observe that although the term "hate speech" is popularly used to mean all speech acts that incite or condone violence against others, scholars interested in the deployment of speech for violent purposes have found the term "hate speech" too broad and difficult to be useful in monitoring the phenomenon. For instance, Saleem et al., (2014) note that the word might refer to the speaker or author's hatred, or his or her desire to make the targets of the speech feel hated, or desire to make others hate the target(s), or the apparent capacity of the speech to increase hatred.

Rosenfeld (2012) observes that much comparative research on hate speech, for examples, has focused on the divide that exists between the American and European approaches to regulating hate speech. While the United States has protection of freedom of expression that stretches well beyond the boundaries of speech that is tolerated in Europe, numerous European countries, including Germany and France, have adopted instead an approach that not only bans forms of speech because of their likelihood to lead to harm, but also for their intrinsic content.

Other societies have developed unique mechanisms to identify and counter hate speech, which may variously combine customary law and formal law. In Somalia for example, where poetry constitutes a popular vehicle for the dissemination of information and ideas, poets who are seen as repeatedly composing poems which community elders consider to be derogatory of individuals or groups, can be banned from composing new work (Stremlau, 2012). In Nigeria, the National Broadcasting Commission has a general guideline on political reportage. Article 3.5.2 of the NBC guideline for example states that: "A media organisation shall not publish or air political adverts; advertorials and sponsored political news that seek to create hatred or incite violence" Article 4.3 of the same guideline states that "A media organisation shall reject any material intended for publication or airing by parties, candidates and other interests that contains hateful or inciting words and messages" while Article 4.4 expect that "A media organisation shall refrain from publishing or airing abusive editorial comments or opinions that denigrate individuals or groups on account of disability, race, ethnicity, tribe, gender or belief."

Centre for Information Technology and Development (CITAD, 2016) sees hate speech as any speech act that is aimed at inciting the audience to denigrate people on the basis of ethnicity, religion, gender, geography and any other socially conceived parameter with the purpose of marginalizing them or placing them at some disadvantage that is contrary to the provisions of the universal rights of the people.

CITAD (2016) reinstates that the dimensions of hate speech include insults of people for their religion, ethnic or linguistic affiliation, contempt against people's place of origin, discrimination on gender and disability basis, abuses or desecration of symbols of cultural or religious practices, ridiculing of traditional or cultural institutions of other people and the spread of falsehood or rumours that demeanor malign or ostracize other people on the basis of religion, ethnicity, gender or place of origin and disability.

Jibrin et al., (2017) also attempt to distinguish hate speech from dangerous speech. According to the authors, hate speech can be harmful, directly or indirectly, or both while dangerous speech has a reasonable chance of catalyzing or amplifying violence by one group against another, given the circumstances in which it is made or disseminated. A speech act in this context includes any form of expression, including images such as drawings or photographs, films, etc. The authors submit that dangerous speech is part of hate speech, which is capable of mobilising people to action.

Benesch (2014) explains that some hate speeches do not increase the risk of psychological damage. Therefore, those concerned with this specific segment of hate speech that invites or condones violence prefer to use the term "dangerous speech" or even "hateful speech." To a large extent, the two terms seem to be mere synonyms describing the same or very similar phenomenon. Benesch (2013) developed a set of guidelines to identify hate or dangerous speech. These guidelines, according to Jibrin et al., (2017) have so far remained the most widely used criteria in identifying hate speech.

The five guidelines include a powerful speaker with a high degree of influence over the audience; an audience that has grievances and fear that the speaker can cultivates; a speech act that is clearly understood as a call to violence; a social or historical context that is propitious for violence, for any of a variety of reasons, including long standing competition between groups for resources, lack of efforts to solve grievances, or previous episodes of violence and lastly, a means of dissemination that is influential in itself, for example because it is the sole or primary source of news for the relevant audience.

The schema does not require that all five elements must be present for the speech act to be classified dangerous. Benesch (2014) also identified the signs of dangerous speech by booking the patterns of wordings and cataloguing what she called the hallmarks of dangerous speech. The signs include the fact that the speech must describe another group as invaders, foreigners, or interlopers; suggest that the other group will besmirch, pollute, or despoil the audience group; dehumanize its targets, e.g. compare them to vermin or insects and the speaker has to use "accusation in a mirror" or assert that the target group posed or poses an existential threat to the audience.

Chapter Summary and Conclusion

The manifestation of hate and dangerous speech in Nigeria constitutes the topic of discussion in this Chapter. The Chapter states that substantial part of the speech was devoted to the historical and current trajectory of Nigeria's development and the challenges; corruption, low literacy rate, infrastructural deficit, citizens' alienation and mistrust for government, poor governance and election fraud. Again, ethno-religious intolerance and hate-speech is so pervasive in Nigeria, that it is sometimes difficult to identify or classify, especially when it is delivered as a form of comedy routine, in book publications and sometimes by the media.

CHAPTER EIGHT
ETHICAL AND LEGAL POSITION OF HATE SPEECH

There are differences in socio-cultural contexts of various societies of the world and that hate speech is both a legal and sociological construct perhaps account for no generally accepted definition of the construct (Oriola, 2019). However, attempts have been made to conceptualise hate speech, though most of the scholarly definitions focus on racial and religious hate. Just like how Oriola (2019) describes hated in the context of human interaction as extreme dislike of persons or groups, on the ground of their racial, ethnic, religious or gender orientation or affiliation. Such extreme dislike may be overt or covert. When it is expressed in speech form or any other non-verbal mode of message display, it becomes covert to the extent of using communication to express such kind of dislike. It is the expression of such extreme dislike which has discriminatory or denigrating consequences that constitutes hate speech (Oriola, 2019).

From the legal perspective, the US legal (2016) describes hate speech as a communication that carries no other meaning than the expression of hatred or incitement to hated against some group of persons defined in terms of race, ethnicity, national origin, gender, religion or sexual orientation especially in circumstances in which the communication provokes violence. This description rightly points generally to communication of information, which is characterised by not only articulated vocal sound speech but also to other communication written, oral and display that are intended to carry meaning to members of the public about certain groups (Aondover, 2023).

It also considers the potential provocation of violence as the result of such communication. However, the definition does not consider expression of hatred to individuals and it limits the potential consequences of hate speech to violence. It should be noted that hate speech affects individuals as it affects groups in the society, especially in the competitive field of politics that is characterised by struggle for supremacy and power. An individual political candidate could be targeted in an expression of hate just as a political group or party.

A bill on 'Prevention of Hate Crime and Hate Speech in South Africa, the summary of which was published in Government Gazette No. 41534 of 29 March 2018, describes an offence of hate speech. Section 1(a) of the Bill describes an offence of hate speech as an intentional communication, publication, propagation or advocacy of any message to:

> One or more persons in a manner that could reasonably by construed to demonstrate a clear intention to (i) be harmful or to incite harm or (ii) promote or propagate hatred, based on one or more of the following grounds: age, albinism, birth, colour, culture, disability, ethnic or social origin, gender or migrant or refugee status, language, nationality, includes intersex or sexual orientation (pp. 4-5).

The Bill also provides that intentional distribution or display of materials capable of being communicated or electronic communication of messages known to constitute hate speech, as provided in the paragraph above through electronic communication system to which members of the public have access and which is directed at a specific individuals who can be victims of such messages, is guilty of an offence of hate speech. However, the Bill provides exceptions to the ingredients that constitute hate speech offence.

Article 19 of the Universal Declaration of Human Right (UDHR) provides and protects the right to freedom of expression and this is given a legal force through Article 19 of the International Covenant on Civil and Political Rights (ICCPR). However, the United Nations (UN) Human Rights Committee (HRC) observes that freedom of expression is not absolute and sets limits to expressions, which may be considered offensive and discriminatory (Oriola, 2019). Therefore, under Article 19(3) of the ICCPR, a state may limit the right to free speech provide that the limitation is provided by law, in pursuance of a legitimate aim and necessary in a democratic society. Hate speech is one of such limitations, which satisfy the three-test condition for restricting free speech. Article 20(2) of the ICCPR describes hate speech as any advocacy of national, racial or religious hatred that constitutes incitement to discrimination, hostility or violence and provides for the prohibition of such expression.

Oguoshi et al., (2019) compare hate speech with free speech doctrine of J.S Mill, which is enshrined in the constitutions of nations. They noted that hate speech is not free speech. Hylton conceived hate speech as negative while free speech is a landmark achievement of democracy. Hence, most developed democracies added a clause on freedom of speech against the use of hate speech. For example, Article 10(2) of the European Convention on Human Rights (ECHR) provides that "the exercise of freedom of expression may be subject to such formalities, conditions, restrictions or penalties as are prescribed by law, the interest of national security for the protection of the reputation or right of others."

Impressively, most doctrines that established freedom of speech and expression in Nigeria added a clause to guard against hate speech, promote human dignity, societal cohesion and peace. For instance, section 39(1) of the 1999 Constitution as amended in 2011 provides that "every person shall be entitled to freedom of expression" Similarly, section 45 provides that nothing in section 39 shall invalidate any law that is reasonably justifiable in a democratic society in the interest of public order, public morality and to protect the rights and freedom of other persons.

Sections 95 and 96 of the 2010 Electoral Act prohibited the use of any language in campaigns that will hurt tribal, religious or sectional feelings. Law of libel and slanders also protect the citizens against hateful utterances. Other legal frameworks that abhor the use of derogatory language in Nigeria are the Political Party Code of Conduct (2013) and the Abuja Accord (2015). Despite these legal frameworks, there has been notable growth in hate speech before, during and after the two general elections held in 2015 and 2019. As noted by Oguoshi et al., (2019) there are, however, existing laws that cater for abuse of freedom or harassment of individuals and groups as pointed out by civil society and mass media groups. The law setting up the National Broadcasting Commission (NBC), Advertising Practitioners Council of Nigeria (APCON), Nigerian Press Council (NPC) and the Nigerian Film and Video Censors Board (NFVCB) filtered out offensive materials and pornography, among others.

Despite the Nigeria Electoral Act of 2010, which spells out detailed provisions specifically barring politically inspired hateful speech, still cases of offensive images of major aspirants, to create a vivid picture of a bad person flourish and have been described by Nigerians as 'one step too far'. Specifically, Section 95 of the Act provides that no political campaign or slogan shall be tainted with abusive language directly or indirectly likely to injure religious, ethnic, tribal or sectional feelings. Similarly, abusive, uncontrolled, slanderous or base language or insinuations or innuendoes designed or likely to provoke violent reaction or emotions shall not be employed or used in political campaigns.

Section 102 of the Act further provides: "Any candidate, person or association who engages in campaigning or broadcasting based on religious, tribal or sectional reason to promote or oppose a particular political party or the election of a particular candidate, is guilty of an offence under this Act and on conviction shall be liable to a maximum fine of N1, 000,000 or imprisonment for twelve months or both." Similarly, paragraph 10(c) of the Guidelines for Political Rallies issued by Independent National Electoral Commission (INEC) of Nigeria also prohibits the use of hate speech and discriminatory rhetoric during campaigns.

Chapter Summary and Conclusion

Ethical and legal position of hate speech formed a topical issue of discuss in this Chapter. There are certain laws in Nigeria that checkmate indiscriminate use of verbal and non-verbal attack on the personality of individuals or group of people. However, despite the legal frameworks that prohibit the use of hateful utterances, the issue of hate speech is still on the increase, which could be as a result of deviance in the manifestation of mental laziness in understanding the laws or the ineffectiveness of such laws.

CHAPTER NINE

FREEDOM OF SPEECH VERSUS HATE SPEECH

Freedom of expression is a natural right individuals enjoy, which is enshrined in local legislation and international human rights law. The historical development of the philosophy of free speech dates back to the ancient Greed when the debate about whether persons other than male landowners should be allowed to speak in public (Oriola, 2019). The advent of mass communication through the invention of printing also attracted repression of expression through licensing laws. However, the popularity of democracy the world over has paved way for international debates leading to legislations and derives. These have resulted in many international legal documents that define and promote free speech (Aondover, 2022).

Notable of these documents (to which Nigeria is a signatory) and their relevant sections are Universal Declaration of Human Rights (UDHR); Article 19, International Covenant on Civil and Political Rights (ICCPR); and Article 19, African Charter on People's and Human Rights (ACPHR). These legal documents are unequivocal on the fundamentality of the right of every person to seek, receive and share any kind of information in any form without any hindrance. Derived from these international legal documents, section 39 (1) of the 1999 Constitution of the Federal Republic of Nigeria as amended provides that "every person shall be entitled to freedom to hold opinions and received and impart ideas and information without interference."

Press freedom and free speech could be considered to be two sides of the same coin as they are both derivatives of the fundamental right to seek, receive and disseminate information without interference. Freedom of the mass media to source for, gather, disseminate information and protect their sources is enshrined in the international human rights law as well as in the Nigerian constitution. All the credence to the right to free speech, provide foundations for freedom of the press. This is because according to Mihajlova et al., in Oriola (2019), the right to free speech includes all stages of identification and dissemination of information, as well as of ideas as processed information, regardless of the format or the media on which they appear.

This suffices then to affirm that press freedom solidly builds on the right to free speech as enshrined in the international laws and conventions. As an extension of the right to free speech, the Nigerian 1999 Constitution expressly provides for freedom of the press in section 39(2) thus: "Without prejudice to the generality of subsection (1) of this section, every person shall be entitled to own, information, ideas and opinions." However, it further provides conditions for ownership of television of wireless broadcasting station. Therefore, within the (Nigerian) national and international levels, legislations about freed speech and press freedom are enshrined in legal documents.

Meanwhile, it should be noted that there is no absolute freedom anywhere in the world. Given the fact that a society is characterised by a web of social interactions, in the course of the exercise of a right by an individual or a group, an infringement on the rights of others may occur. This consideration and that of national security are often adduced for limitations to human rights, including the right to such regulations and control lead to censorship restraints or limits on publication. One of such limits which have attracted concerted focus is restrictions on hate speech. The need to promote equality and discourage discrimination is provided in Articles 1, 2, and 7 of the UDHR and Article 2(1), Article 20(2) and 26 of the ICCR. For instance, Article 20(2) of the ICCPR places the obligation on States to legally prohibit "any advocacy of national, racial or religious hatred that constitutes incitement to discrimination, hostility or violence." This is an express international human rights requirement for the prohibition of hate speech.

The Nigerian constitution does not expressly provide restrictions on hate speech but in section 42, it provides for the right to freedom of discrimination to which a person may be subjected expressly or by application of law or any executive or administrative action of government based on the person's place of origin, sex, religion or political opinion. However, the fact that the provision for non-discrimination in the Nigerian constitution focuses on the application of law and government actions but not on the expressive activities of individuals, groups and the mass media makes this provision inadequate to address the issue of hate speech. It should be noted that many countries of the world have built on international human rights law to conceptualise and expressly restrict expression of hated in any form of their legal documents.

According to Oriola (2019), Britain, Germany, Austria, the Netherlands, India and South Africa have enacted and enforced hate speech legislation.

In Poland for instance, there are prohibitions of hate speech in criminal law and civil laws as well as administrative law (Article 19, 2018), Articles 119(1), 256(1) and 257 of the Polish Penal Code are provisions in the country's criminal law that restrict hate speech. The Polish Construction Law and the Law on National and Ethnic Minorities and Regional Language are relevant administrative measures against hate speech. Article 23 and 24 of the Polish Civil Code prohibits hate speech and provides persons to demand for civil actions to seek redress. As regards media regulation on hate speech, Poland's Broadcasting Act of 1992 specifically prohibits the broadcast of content of hate and discrimination against persons and groups based on their identifiable features (Article 19, 2018).

In South Africa, the debate about restriction of hate speech has attracted legislative processes with the introduction of 'Prevention and Combating of Hate Crimes and Hate Speech Bill' in the National Assembly on March 29, 2018, the explanatory summary of which was published in Government Gazette (No. 41543 of 29 March 2018) (Republic of South Africa, 2018).

Nigeria needs to take the debate on hate speech beyond mere campaign and advance steps towards its legislation. This becomes necessary due to the growing importance of the discourse, to the growing democracy as a multi-ethnic, multi-cultural and multi-lingual society. The potential damaging effect of hate speech on the victims and the consequences it is capable of wielding on the democratic system of the Nigerian state suffice that adequate legal and administrative attention be paid to the issue. The need to set boundaries to the legal guarantee of free speech and press freedom necessitate express legislation on the issue on one hand. On the other hand, the need for legal and administrative conceptualization of hate speech for its distinction from insults, slander, libel, satire, comedy, propaganda, criticisms and legitimate protests against government policies is of necessity for the present government not to be guilty of political witch-hunting.

Nwokoro (2019) observes that defending freedom of speech means defending all speech equally, even when such a speech may be regarded as offensive like hate speech. Drawing from this perspective, such examples of hate speech includes name-calling, racial slurs, reproach to gender equality, symbols but some symbols like swastika, burning crosses, etc are still debated upon whether they are hate speech or not, especially depending on the context it was used. In America and the United Kingdom, citizens believe that freedom of speech when used too freely without checking what people say, could lead to hate speech. This is because; people will be too free when expressing themselves. Therefore in other not to let people abuse freedom of speech, John Stuart Mill, a great defender of free speech said that some rules of conduct must be imposed as freedom of speech has become a loophole exploited with impunity by trolls, racists and ethnic cleansing advocates (*The Guardian*, March, 22, 2018).

According to the Nwokoro (2019) freedom of speech is the right to express opinion without Government restraint. It is a democratic ideal that dates back to ancient Greece. The First Amendment, which was adopted on 15 December, 1791 to the American constitution guarantees free speech but there are limits placed on this freedom in the USA, Nigeria as in other modern democracies. These limits are to prevent people from making statements that can be detrimental to the peaceful coexistence of members of the said community. Freedom can be restricted, if its exercise will cause direct and imminent harm on people. The forms of speech that are not protected under the First Amendment include those that violate the physical, emotional and mental well-being of others especially children. Similarly, freedom of speech does not apply when pornography; plagiarism of copyrighted material; defamation (slander and libel); true threats and speeches inciting illegal action or soliciting others to commit crimes are not covered.

Olornyomi (2018, p. 265) states that when talking of freedom of speech principles, it is good to draw a line between responsible criticism and hate speech. He went onto states that 'that we are defending freedom of speech does not mean people will express themselves without them knowing their boundaries so also is hate speech, therefore, responsible criticism on those in power should not be seen as a form of hate speech'. This is not the case with the present democratic dispensation in Nigeria that sees hate speech as any insult, legitimate protests against government policies or comedic jibes with little regard as to why it is so (Abimbola, 2017). In addition, Nwokoro (2019) thinks that the free speech principle tends to favour those in power and tilts against those out of power or the governed. This scenario is not far from the truth as to what takes place in Nigeria.

On the part of the mass media in general with particular reference to any story that is published in the newspaper, they should be guided by what the law and Human Right Organisation (HRO) say about hate speech. This is to help newspapers prevent a lawsuit and not to be regarded as a 'hatist' medium. In a survey conducted by National Telecommunication and Information Administration (NTIA) in Nwokoro (2019) reveals that individuals have used telecommunications to disseminate messages of hate and bigotry to a wide audience. Thus, in an ideal situation, the media in Nigeria should help act as a means of checking the spread of hate speech and not act as promoters of hate speech in the society. This is so because section 45 of the Nigeria 1999 Constitution also limits freedom of expression by stating that 'nothing in section 37, 38, 39, 40 and 41 shall invalidate any law that is reasonably justifiable in a democratic society.'

Chapter Summary and Conclusion

Indeed, freedom of expression is universally acknowledged as both a fundamental and foundational human right. Freedom of expression is a natural right individuals enjoy, which is enshrined in local legislation and international human rights law. The Chapter submits that the historical development of the philosophy of free speech dates back to the ancient Greed when the debate about whether persons other than male landowners should be allowed to speak in public. The advent of mass communication through the invention of printing also attracted repression of expression through licensing laws. However, the popularity of democracy the world over has paved way for international debates leading to legislations and derives. These have resulted in many international legal documents that define and promote free speech.

CHAPTER TEN
THE EFFECTS OF HATE SPEECH

Public discourse about hate speech has been gathering momentum in recent times, especially as the present President, Muhammadu Buhari-led administration is calling attention to it and launching campaigns to Nigeria, media practitioners have lent their voices to its conceptualisation (Oriola, 2019). For instance, Adelakun (2017) observes that the period of the 2015 electioneering campaign in Nigeria marks the resurgence of hate speech due to the widespread vitriolic political propaganda among political actors. The broadcast of a documentary considered hateful to the presidential candidate of the All Progressive Congress (APC), Muhammadu Buhari on the Africa Independent Television (AIT) drew the attention of his party, resulting in a petition to the National Broadcasting Commission. The petition labeled the aired content 'hate broadcast' for which AIT was to be sanctioned. With the victory of the APC candidate leading to his office as the president, the campaign against hate speech has been under the focus of the administration (Aondover, 2021).

The campaign is now beyond the social media coverage of issues and has extended to the mainstream media messages. As Adelakun (2017) observes, there is a need for a legal and administrative conceptualisation of hate speech for the purpose of boundary setting so that mere social media commentaries, as well as mainstream media messages that constitute insults, slander, libel, comedy, propaganda, criticism and legitimate protests against government policies, are not misconstrued as hate speech. The impetus for the campaign could be derived from the fact that Nigeria is a multi-ethnic, multi-lingual, and culturally sensitive society where language has contextual meaning. An expression that is permissible in one culture may be considered offensive in another and as such, the social and political uses of expressions need to be considered. This could be the reason why Waltman and Haas in Oriola (2019) note that hate speech could serve social and political functions in a democratic society with implications on intimidation of members of an out-group on the basis of their racial, ethnic, religious, or sexual orientations. This implies that intimidation is a necessary ingredient of hate speech. The authors also observed that the promotion of violence against members of the out-group is one of the intentions of the users of hate expression.

In tandem with US Legal (2016), this brings into consideration, violence as a possible consequence of hate speech. The third ingredient of hate speech considered by the authors is that it is used to mentally and psychologically construct a collective form of memory through belief teaching and orientation among members of the in-group. Fourthly, hate speech serves recruitment purposes for group members. On the effects of hate speech, Brown (2017, p. 420) asserts that attention to its implications on "harm, dignity, security, healthy cultural dialogue, democracy, and legitimacy are fundamental." It is harmful to individual and group victims alike.

Corroborating Brown on the harmful effect of hate speech, Oriola (2019) states that hate speech expresses advocates, encourages, promotes, or incites hatred of a group of individuals distinguished by a particular feature or set of features that create discord in the community, harms the target group and infringes upon equality. Citing examples of Britain, Germany, Austria, the Netherlands, India, and Post-apartheid South Africa, he observes that political discourse and competition are healthier in climes that enact and enforce hate speech legislation. This opinion points to incitement, disunity, and inequality as harmful effects of the expression of hate, the consequence of which denigrates the victim, based on their identifiable features and disrupts the political process.

Oriola (2019) remarks that hate speech causes emotional and psychological discomfort to the victims; diminishes social and entrepreneurial mobility by promoting inequality; leads to behaviour, such as drug abuse and alcoholism, and potentially leads to hate crime, which has serious consequences for societal peace, order, and security. More relevant is the author's opinion that hate speech impedes the principle of the free marketplace of ideas in a democracy as it promotes social and political exclusion against certain individuals and groups termed as out-group in Waltman and Ashely's (2017) classification.

Chapter Summary and Conclusion

The Chapter discussion was on the effects of hate speech. In this direction, the effects of political activities in developing countries and particularly Nigeria have shown that hate speech has become more vivid in the successive democratic dispensation than the previous ones thereby keeping the citizens more divided. Within this context, the Chapter submits that the main mission of journalism is basically to be a fourth estate for good speech and to serve the public interest by reporting the truth, with positive language, in total independence and with a sense of responsibility, without any form of hate speech.

CHAPTER ELEVEN

INSTANCES AND CRITICISM OF HATE SPEECH IN NIGERIA

The 2015 and 2019 elections were very keen to the extent that an alliance of opposition parties was formed to produce All Progressives Congress (APC) in a strong bid to dislodge the Peoples Democratic Party (PDP) that had been in power since 1999. Findings from the monitoring of the media coverage of these elections showed that there were cases of sponsorship of hate advertorials by the then Ekiti State governor, Ayodele Fayose who, on January 19, 2015, ran adverts on the front pages of national dailies such as *The Daily Sun, The Guardian* and *The Punch* titled "Nigeria Be Warned". In the advert, satirical reference was made to Buhari, the presidential candidate of the APC, that given his age and speculated illness and frail nature, he might die in office should he win, according to *Sahara Reporters* of January 19, 2015.

Additionally, section 95 of the Electoral Act 2010 disapproves of hate campaigns by stipulating that: (1) A political campaign or slogan shall not be tainted with abusive language directly or indirectly likely to injure religious, ethnic, tribal, or sectional feelings. (2) Abusive, intemperate, slanderous, or base language or insinuations or innuendoes designed or likely to provoke violent reactions or emotions shall not be employed or used in political campaigns. Yet, there were other instances of lack of discretion on the part of the media in the countdown to the 2015 and 2019 elections, in terms of inappropriate language use and inciting headlines. This was evident in the outcome of the monitoring of 12 National newspapers like *Daily Trust, The Nation, The Guardian, The Punch, The Guardian, Vanguard, Daily Independent, National Mirror, Leadership, Nigerian Tribune, ThisDay,* and *Daily Champion* (Arogundade, 2019).

Findings by IPC (2015) reveal that stories capable of inciting one section against the other were recorded 45 times during this monitoring period while hate speech featured 8 times despite these provisions. A total of 117 reports were recorded in these categories in the six months at an average of about

20 per month across the 12 selected national print media. The documented inciting headlines also include the following: APC presidential candidate is a fundamentalist- Clarke (*ThisDay*, Jan. 17, 2015, page 15); will you allow history to repeat history itself? Enough of state burials (*Daily Sun*, Jan. 19, 2015, page 1); we're set for war – PAC (*Nigerian Tribune*, November 22, 2019), among others.

The Hate Speech Bill which was proposed by the Nigerian Senate prescribed death by hanging for any person found guilty of any form of hate speech that results in the death of another person. The 'Hate Speech Bill' was sponsored by Senator Aliyu Sabi Abdullahi of Niger State and has death by hanging, inserted as capital punishment for offenders. The Bill seeks to "eliminate" hate speech and discourage harassment on the grounds of ethnicity, religion, or race among others. It prescribes stiff penalties for offences such as "ethnic hatred." "Any person who uses, publishes, presents, produces, plays, provides, distributes, or directs the performance of any material, written or visual, which is threatening, abusive or insulting or involves the use of threatening, abusive or insulting words, commits an offence."

However, a barrage of criticisms has trailed the introduction of the bill, with many of the views that it was aimed at hunting critics of the government. The bill stated clearly a penalty for those who are found guilty of any form of hate speech that results in the death of another person after judicial processes in a Federal High Court. *Critical sections of the society like the mass media, civil society, pressure groups, the academia, writers, and creative or performing artists who expectedly will bear the main brunt of the obnoxious law have been curiously and dangerously indifferent, as only a few voices have raised the alarm.* The critics of this penalty thought that death penalty should have been provided as the punishment when someone or a group is responsible for the deaths of other people. After all, the present law says 'if you do anything that results in the death of another person and it is proven beyond reasonable doubt that you caused the death of that person, the penalty is death by hanging.' In a very damming editorial on March 19, 2018, *The Punch* criticized the bill in the following words:

> Purveying or inciting hatred is bad, but viewed from all perspectives, this is a bad law being proposed by persons so unfamiliar and uncomfortable with the practices and nuances of fundamental rights and democracy. Not even in his first term as a military head of state did President Muhammadu

> Buhari propose such heavy jail terms and fines against the exercise of free speech and media freedom. The infamous anti-media Decree 4 that headlined the military junta he led in 1984-85 came far short of imposing millions of naira in fines or prescribing the death penalty. Neither did the British colonial masters who drafted and enforced a succession of sedition and anti-press laws contemplate silencing freed speech with the death penalty (p. 45).

Like other critics, it is noted that the Bill sits at odds with provisions on basic fundamental rights outlined in Chapter IV of the 1999 Constitution, especially Sections 38 and 39 that guarantee the freedom of thought, conscience, and religion; and freedom of expression and the press, respectively. The basic law and enabling legislation, also sufficiently prohibit the abuse of such rights and discrimination against persons or groups on account of race, ethnicity, or faith. Nigerian Senator, Shehu Sani, as quoted by *Sahara Reporters* (2018) argues that the law against hate speech will be used against free speech, that it would be a threat to democracy and freedom of speech, and Nigerians should fight and reject it. Believing that the bill would be used to intimidate and arrest critics of the government, Sani states that "many critics and social media enthusiasts will be filled with the gallows. Our condemned cells in the prisons will be filled with bloggers, critics, and perceived political opponents. We must fight hate speech, hate speech is a real threat to the peace, unity, and order of a nation, but we must protect free speech. Free speech is the shield of the oppressed."

Chapter Summary and Conclusion

In this Chapter, instances and criticism of hate speech in Nigeria was given due consideration. Owing to social diversities, hate and other related speeches tend to vary across time and space and possibly constrain by existential societal realities. As earlier stated in this Chapter, the uneasy relationship across federating groups in Nigeria, remains are a definite attribute of Africa's suppose power house. The prevailing trend equally accords ethnic entrepreneurs as well as the avenue to heat of the polity and promotes prejudice in the society. Therefore, both individuals and the society disapprove the use of hate speech as well as the legal frameworks.

CHAPTER TWELVE

THEORETICAL POSTULATIONS OF HATE SPEECH AND VIOLENCE IN NIGERIA

Hate speech is any speech, conduct, gesture, writing, or display which could incite people to violence or execute a prejudicial action. Essentially such speeches rob others of their dignity and sense of order (Mrabure, 2015). United Nations Committee on the Elimination of Racial Discrimination (2016) in its interpretation of the law, notes that hate speech offences include:

> (a) all dissemination of ideas based on racial or ethnic superiority or hatred by whatever means; (b) incitement to hatred, contempt, or discrimination against members of a group on the ground of their race, colour, descent, national or ethnic origin; (c) threats or incitement to violence against persons or group on the grounds in (b) above and (d) expression of insults, ridicule or slander of persons or groups or justification of hatred, contempt or discrimination on the in (b) above when it amounts to incitement to hatred or discrimination and (e) participation in organisation and activities which will promote and incite radical discrimination and violence (p. 35).

As a term, hate speech can be said to have put down its roots in Nigeria since the 2015 election campaign (Ezeibe, 2015). To be specific, the term seemed to have gained public attention in Nigeria after a documentary aired on African Independent Television (AIT) about an All Progressive Congress (APC) Presidential election. Due to perceived hostility and partisanship from the transmitting station, the documentary was later described as a 'hate broadcast.' Hate speech seems mostly associated with power elites. Some utterances from political leaders, wealthy persons, religious heads and others who can be regarded as role mentors have been regarded as hate speeches

(Okunna, 2018). Some examples of such instances made by leaders in Nigeria and reported in the press are as follows:

'*Buhari would likely die in office if elected*, recall that Murtala Muhammed, Sani Abacha and Umaru Yar'Adua, *all former heads of state from the Northwest like, Buhari, had died in office*' – The Governor of Ekiti State, Peter Ayodele Fayose, January 19, 2015, *ThisDay* and other national dailies.

'*Wetin him dey find again? Him dey drag with him pikin mate, old man wey no get brain, him brain don die pata pata* – what else *is he (Buhari) after, contesting with people young enough to be his children. The old man who lacks gumption; he is completely brain dead.*' – Former First Lady, Patience Jonathan, at a PDP political party rally in Kogi State, Reported by *The Express News*, 4th March, 2014.

'*God willing, by 2015 something will happen. They either conduct a free and fair election or they go a very disgraceful way. If what happened in 2011 should again happen in 2015, by the grace of God, the dog and the baboon would all be soaked in blood.*' – Presidential Candidate of Congress for Progressive Change, General Muhammadu Buhari, Reported by Lika Binniyat in *Vanguard Newspaper* on May, 15th 2012.

The emphasis highlighted in italic merely indicates the depth of negative passion resentment for an individual which extended to his group and the levity with which death as a mode of dismissal is taken. Yet such hate speech needs media for widespread circulation to gain prominence. Without the media, hate speech could fail to come alive (Okunna, 2018).

Within the theoretical postulations, Lazarsfeld and Katz's Two-Step Flow Theory was first introduced by Lazarsfeld et al., in 1944 to study the process of decision-making during a Presidential election campaign. In this direction, there is a support for the direct influence of media messages on voting intentions. Katz and Lazarsfeld developed the two-step flow theory of mass communication and this theory asserts that information from the media moves in two distinct stages. First, individuals (opinion leaders) who pay close attention to the mass media and its messages receive the information. Opinion leaders pass on their interpretations in addition to the actual media content. The term 'personal influence' was coined to refer to the process of intervening between the media's direct message and the audience's ultimate reaction to that message. Opinion leaders are quite influential in getting people to change their attitudes and behaviours and are quite similar to those they influence. The two-step flow theory has improved the understanding of how the mass media influence decision-making.

The theory refined the ability to predict the influence of media messages on audience behaviour, and it helped explain why certain media campaigns may have failed to alter audience attitudes or behaviour. The two-step flow theory gave way to the multi-step flow theory of mass communication. Although the empirical methods behind the two-step flow of communication were not perfect, the theory did provide a very believable explanation for information flow. The opinion leaders do not replace media, but rather guide discussions of media, which at times lead to issues of hate speeches.

Lazarsfeld et al., in Hassan (2020) discover that most voters got their information about the candidates from other people who read about the campaign in the newspapers, not directly from the media. They conclude that word-of-mouth transmission of information plays an important role in the communication process and that mass media have only a limited influence on most individuals. Since opinion leaders pass on their interpretations in addition to the actual media content, the manifestation of hate speeches on the pages of newspapers and how the opinion leaders tag meaning to words in Nigeria like (Gandollar instead of Ganduje) would affect the electoral victory when such interpretations are in a negative direction.

Castells' Theory of Network Society examines the concept of the network to a high level of abstraction, utilizing it as a concept that depicts macro-level tendencies associated with the social organization in informational capitalism. He expresses the role of networks in social theory as follows dominant functions and processes in the information age are increasingly organised around networks. Networks constitute the hate speech morphology in societies, and the diffusion of networking logic substantially modifies the operation and outcomes in processes of production, experience, power, and culture. Understanding the societal context of such networks entails returning to the political economy of the social transformation of capitalist society. An analytical concept network is abstract and thus unable to frame the interpretation of real-life networks, whereas theoretical concept network is an excellent crystallization of the social morphology of informational capitalism.

As an upshot of the latter, the concept of network society has a certain intellectual appeal, even if it looks almost as if the formal description of the concept of the network was needed only to legitimate its use as a metaphor. Concerning the hardcore of the metaphor, the book comes to the true message of Castellsian political economy (where politicians metaphorically used negative words to refer to other opposition), and the network in its paradigmatic form is about the nodes and connections of powerful financial and economic institutions, which allow the flows of values in pursuit of the newspapers' accumulation of capital. This implies that 'network' in Castells' social theory is not an analytical concept but rather a powerful metaphor that served to capture the new social morphology of the capitalist system. In this context, the morphological manifestation of hate speech in the discourse of information society gain its momentum; it went out of intellectual fashion as well as political agenda and gave its place to the visions of the creative and or smart society. For instance, in Nigeria, the phrase 'change begins with me' is often used metaphorically and polemical.

Although the critics, who looked at the theories of the information society suspiciously as ideological constructs, created for political decisions, rather than instruments for understanding the social reality. Therefore, Castells believes that McLuhan's dictum "the medium is the message" could be adequately applied in the way hate speeches flourish in newspapers' content. In this perspective, there is a network (politicians and newspaper organisations), which often creates a powerful metaphor that aptly portrayed hate speech as a social morphology of information capitalism (Doda, 2015).

Durkheim's Social Fact and Weber's Social Action or Relations Theory emphasizes the importance of social collectivity and its determination over individual consciousness, pointing out concepts like *sui generis* of social facts, function, causality, generality, etc. Weber's on the other hand based his argument on concepts such as meaning, social action, interpretation, methodological individualism, etc. The book depicts both theorists to understand the social order or social reality of hate speech at the theoretical level and the approach to this social reality focused attention on individualistic autonomy in terms of ideas and desires vis-à-vis social regularity.

Weber approached the problem of social regulation through the question of how this regularity becomes possible out of the chaos of individualistic ambiguity. In this manner, he searched for the underlying rules and principles in this order. According to Weber, social continuity or social order is constructed at the individualistic consciousness level through how social actors assign meaning to their actions. Weber in Doda (2015) proposes that the reason behind regular actions is the meaning that individuals attribute to their actions. Like the action towards hate speech, the acting individual attaches a subjective meaning to his behaviour, which can be overt or covert, omission or acquiescence that is concerned with 'meaning-attributed-action' within society.

For Weber, people give meaning not only to their behaviour but also to behaviour of other people in their reciprocal relationships, because the action of each takes account of that of others. Weber understands social regularity as the harmony of individualistic social actions and meanings individuals attribute to the actions of other people. Therefore, individuals' attribution of meaning to action and social relationships gives social life its regularity; otherwise, social action would be impossible. In Weberian analysis, these regularities in social and individualistic levels merge in social action. Unlike Weber, Durkheim, when considering social order, essentially evaluates it as a whole, not as a set of individualistic actions or unique particularities.

Durkheim proposes that to understand how society thinks of itself and of its environment one must consider the nature of the society and not that of the individuals. According to Durkheim, social continuity arises from the domination of social regulations over the ambiguity of the individualistic infinite and indeterminate psychological needs and desires.

As "hate speech is a reality *sui generis*" in the case of the Durkheimian approach. For Durkheim, because individualistic needs are infinite, society imposes limits on human desires. In this manner, Durkheim's idea of social action refers to "*sui generis* of social facts," namely, the determination of "external conditions," which implies not a probability but a certainty. On the other hand, in the Weberian sense, social action has to do with 'not a certainty but probability'. For example, when Weber explains types of action orientation, he defines 'usage' as an orientation toward social action that occurs regularly, it will be called 'usage' (*Brauch*) insofar as the probability of its existence within a group is based on nothing but actual practice. As one can see, for Weber, ideas (hate speech) can assume a role in social change. On the other hand, Durkheim demonstrates that individualistic ideas and thoughts (hate speech) can never affect the path of the existing social order.

The Functional Theory of Campaign Discourse, according to Doda (2015) explains the functional theory of campaign discourse, which renders a helpful scheme to classify and synthesize political advertising. He adds that elections are intrinsically competitive, political actors deploy campaign messages, which include advertising to present a more preferable image of them. They use political ads to acclaim themselves, positive statements about their credentials as the better candidate; attack an opponent's credentials, or defend with reputations against an opponents' attack through media platforms. Candidates use two functions for themes of policy: policy themes can discuss actions or ideas related to governmental action related to past deeds, plans, and general goals. Character: character themes can discuss the candidate's perceived qualities related to personal qualities, leadership abilities, and values or principles. It would be interesting to see the extent of the use of self-acclaim, attacks, ethnic insult, blotch campaigns, religious divisiveness, or issue-based topics relating to economic, social, cultural, and political policies.

For instance, in the 2015 and 2019 elections, there were cases of sponsorship of hate advertorials by the then Ekiti State governor, Ayodele Fayose who, on January 19, 2015, ran adverts on the front pages of national dailies such as *The Daily Sun, The Guardian* and *The Punch* titled: "Nigeria Be Warned". In the advert, satirical reference was made to Buhari, the presidential candidate of the APC, that given his age and speculated illness and frail nature, he might die in office should he win, according to *Sahara Reporters* of January 19, 2015. As corroborated by Roberts (2013) elections are intrinsically competitive, political actors deploy campaign messages, which include advertising to present a more preferable image that comes in form of hate advertorial, which serves the research goal in understanding how politicians synthesize political advertising using hate speech.

Critical Discourse Analysis Theory provides a reality that can be represented either truthfully or falsely in language. The theory assumes that it is possible to represent reality in an unmediated, neutral form; critique is then based on whether the ideal is attained or not. Neutral representations are opposed to ideological representations, which are deemed to 'distort reality.' Ideology is, accordingly, conceptualised in negative terms, as the opposite of 'truth.' Critical Discourse Analysis Theory describes and analyse how the structure and content of the text encode ideas and the relation among the idea itself that is present in the text, systematically. Here, it connotes how hate speech and language, dialects, and acceptable statements are used in a particular medium across different audiences. The theory looks at discourse among people who share the same speech conventions. It also refers to the linguistics of language use as a way of understanding interactions in a social context, specifically, the analysis of occurring connected speech or written discourse like APC presidential candidate is a fundamentalist- Clarke (*ThisDay*, Jan. 17, 2015, page 15).

Furthermore, Fairclough in Omidiora *et al.*, (2019) argues that social practice has various orientations economic, political, cultural, ideological, and discourse may be implicated in all of these without any of them being reducible to discourse. The author further states that in this line, discursive practice is constitutive in both conventional and creative ways: it contributes to reproducing society (social identities, social relationships, systems of knowledge and belief) as it is, yet also contributes to transforming society. In this context, the theory is apt as it provides a reality that can be represented either truthfully or falsely in language.

Critical Race Theory (CRT) also provides a compelling structure by which media concepts and hate speech can be analyzed and understood. According to Odera (2015) CRT indicates that media use phrases sponsored by politicians that refer to other opposition groups from descriptions that are not merely rhetorical but pedestals on which hate speech flourishes (Rasaq et al., 2017). Theoretically, critical race theory underscores that violent political rhetoric is capable of producing the same psychological dynamics as violent entertainment (Rasaq et al., 2017).

Through critical race theory, framing words on the assumption that a subtle change in the wording of the description of a situation might affect how the audience interprets the situation. This portends that media coverage can help influence how people think about candidates, events, and other issues. As a result, framing refers to the impact of news coverage on the weight assigned to specific issues in making political judgments. This means that the media may draw more attention to some aspects of political life like the elections and the aftermath at the expense of others (Rasaq et al., 2017). The interpretation of critical race theory is that in choosing and displaying news, editors, newsroom staff and broadcasters play an important part in shaping political reality. Consequently, readers learn not only about given issues but how much importance to attach to that issue from the amount of information in a news story and its position.

In response to that Critical Race Theory is used to support a legal-structural response to hate speech. It aims to transform the relationship between race, law, and power. CRT recognizes that the vested interests of the economic-political elite shape racial and ethnic stratification. Thus, the theory provides a compelling structure by which media concepts and hate speech can be analysed and understood. This indicates that media use phrases sponsored by politicians that refer to other opposition groups from descriptions that are not merely rhetorical but pedestals on which hate speech emanate. Arguably, some literature challenged the dominant ideology of Critical Race Theory based on race and racism, the social construction of race storytelling and counter storytelling as well as the notion of white supremacy.

Chapter Summary and Conclusion

Theoretical postulation of hate speech and violence in Nigeria is a concluding Chapter that interrogates the position of theories to better understand the issue of hate speech. In this contestation, theories abound in the discussion of hate speech, which shape the understanding that provide explanation within the premise of theoretical arguments as regard to the disturbing issue of hate speech in Nigeria.

REFERENCES

Adegoju, A. (2015). Person deixis as discursive practice in Nigeria's "June 12" conflict rhetoric. *Ghana Journal of Linguistic*, 3(1), 45-64.

Ademilokun, M. (2015). Discursive strategies in selected political rally campaigns of 2011 elections in Southwestern Nigeria. *International Journal of Society, Culture & Language*, 3(1), 120-132.

Adibe, J. (2015). Fayose's advert: Offensive or hate speech? Adapted from a paper presented at a roundtable on hate speech organized by the Kukah Centre, Abuja.

Adibe, J. (2018). Ethnicity, hate speech and nation-building. http://www.gamji.com/adibe/adibe19.htm, 2019.

Alakali, T. T., Faga, H. P. & Mbursa, J. (2017). Audience perception of hate speech and foul language in the social media in Nigeria: implications for morality and law. *Academicus International Scientific Journal*, 3(2), 161-177.

Aondover, E. M. & Muhammad, M. (2018). Perceptions of hate speech among journalists. *International Journal of Research and Scholarly Communication*, 2(1), 88-102.

Aondover, E. M. (2021). Content Analysis of Hate Speech in the 2019 General Elections in Three Nigerian Newspapers. *American Journal of Multidisciplinary Research in Africa*, 1(3), 1-9.

Aondover, E. M. (2022). Interpretative Phenomenological Analysis of Hate Speech among Editors of Daily Trust, The Nation and The Guardian Newspapers in Nigeria. Konfrontasi Journal: Culture, Economy and Social Changes, 9(2), 216-226. DOI: https://doi.org/10.33258/konfrontasi2.v9i2.209.

Aondover, E. M. (Ed). (2023). *Hate speech on social media: A global approach*. Social media narratives and reflections on hate speech in Nigeria. In Difatima, B. Labcom Communication & Arts, 255-275.

Arogundade, L. (2019). *Media and elections: professional responsibilities of journalists*. Lagos. Tentacle Communication.

Batta, N. Mboho, M. & Batta, H. (2016). Political Advertising and Electioneering in Nigeria: An Analysis of 2015 General Election Newspaper Advertisements. *European Journal of Business and Management*, 10(1), 18-17.

Bello, K. (2015). Hate speech will be considered an act of terrorism – Osinbajo. Today. NG. https://www.today.ng/news/nigeria/5294/hate-speech-considered-terrorism.

Benesch, S. (2013). Dangerous speech: A proposal to prevent group violence, dangerous speech project. World Policy Institute, New York, no 3. http://www.worldpolicy.org/sites/default/files/dangerous%20seech%guidelines%20Benesch%20january%2020.pdf.

Benesch, S. (2014) Countering dangerous speech. New ideas for genocide prevention, working paper on dangerous speech project.

CITAD (2016). Traders of hate in search of votes: tracking dangerous speech in Nigeria's 2015 election campaign, CITAD, Kano.

Independent National Electoral Commission, (2015). Report on the 2015 and 2019 general elections. http://www.inec.com.

International Press Centre, (2018). *The resource manual on elections and democratic accountability reporting* (ICP & EU-SDGN, 2018).

Jibrin, I., Pate, U., Charmaine, P. Agbanyin, O. & Bagu, O. (2017). The escalation of hate and dangerous speech in the build up to the 2015 election and the imperative of strengthening the broadcast code. National Broadcasting Commission Draft Report, July Tapestry Consulting, Abuja.

Kukah, H. (2016). Hate speech, social media and 2015 general elections in Nigeria. www.pointbanknews.com/hatespeech,socialmediaand2015elections.

Nwokoro, C. I. (eds). (2019). Perspectives on the use of radio in countering hate speech and violence in Benue and Delta States. *Fake news and hate speech: narratives of political instability*. (6th ed.). Canada University Press, Concord Ontario, Canada.

Ogbuoshi, L. I., Oyeleke, A. S. & Folorunsho, O.M. (eds). (2019). Opinion leaders' perspectives on hate speech and fake news reporting and Nigeria's political stability. *Fake news and hate speech: narratives of political instability*. (6th ed.). Canada University Press, Concord Ontario, Canada.

Omidiora, O., Ajiboye, E. & Abioye, T. (eds). (2019). Beyond fun, media entertainment, politics and development in Nigeria. The marriage of the popular and the political: A critical analysis of Nigerian hip hop music in electoral campaign discourse. Malthouse Press Limited.

Oriola, O. M. (eds). (2019). Mainstream media reporting of hate speech and press freedom in Nigeria politics. *Fake news and hate speech: narratives of political instability.* (6th ed.). Canada University Press, Concord Ontario, Canada.

Oso, L. (2015). Press and politics in Nigeria: on whose side? Lagos: LASU Inaugural Lecture Series, Lagos State University.

Oso, L. (2018). *These are interesting times.* A welcome address at the 5th Annual Conference of the Association of Communication Scholars and Professionals of Nigeria (ACSPN), Asaba.

Pate, U. A. & Jibril, A. (eds). (2018). *Professional safety and security among Nigerian journalists.* in Popoola, M. & Oboah, G.E. Political economy of media operations. (1st ed.). Franco-ola Printers.

Pate, U. A. & Oso, L. (eds). (2017). *Multiculturalism, diversity, reporting conflict in Nigeria.* (1st ed.).Ibadan: Evan Brothers Nigeria Publishing Limited.

Pate, U.A. (2015). *Issues in media and national integration in Nigeria.* Lagos: African Resource Communications Ltd.

Popoola, T. (2019). *Parrot journalism. A professional guide in investigative journalism.* Lagos. Diamond Publications Limited.

Rasaq, A. Udende, P. Ibrahim, A. & Oba, L. (2017). Media, politics, and hate speech: a critical discourse analysis. *e-Academia Journal*, 6(1), 240-252.

Rosenfeld, M. (2012). Hate speech in Constitutional Jurisprudence. In the content and context of hate speech, Cambridge University Press.

Suleiman, H. & Owolabi, E. (2018). Hate speech and its harms: A communicative perspective. *Journal of Communication*, 47(1), 4-19.

The Punch, (2017, June 20). 2015 and 2019 general elections in Nigeria.

United Nations Committee on the Elimination of Racial Discrimination (2016). General recommendation on combating racist hate speech", CERD/C/GC/35.